AWAKENED

MEETINGS WITH INDIAN SAINTS

D1563405

MICHAEL O'CALLAGHAN

SPIRIT WINGS PUBLISHING
P. O. Box 92694
Austin, Texas 78709-2694
www.spiritwingspublishing.com

Cataloging in Publication Data
O'Callaghan, Michael, 1948–
Awakened: Meetings with Indian Saints/Michael O'Callaghan, PhD

Austin, TX: Spirit Wings Publishing
p.   cm.
Includes Glossary, Reading List.

1. Spiritual Life   2. Gurus   3. Saints
4. Enlightenment   5. Title   6. Hinduism
ISBN 0-9752885-0-4
BL 1241.48 .O3 2004   294.509   200409491

Printed in USA
at Morgan Printing in Austin, Texas

Dedicated to all of my gurus,
to my extraordinary, ever-loyal, ever-laughing
Irish clan of brothers and sisters,
to my daughter,
and to my friends.

CONTENTS

Acknowledgments

To my sister Sheila, my brother Tommy, my brother-in-law Arthur, and my daughter Vera for their careful reading, encouragement, and helpful comments on the manuscript. To my sister Patricia for her excellent advice as librarian and writer.

To my friends Karen Atamian, Linda Lella, Rush Barnes, R.K. Panditi, Michael Kannan, Barbara Foley, Jean Marie McLain, Gretel Baacke, Mary Brenner, and Sandie BonSell for their incisive comments and generous reading of the manuscript in its various phases. To Judy Kew for her expert editing and infinite patience.

To Terry Sherrell, Elizabeth Lary and Stephen Bright for their artistry in layout and cover design.

To all my meditating colleagues who, against all odds, make group meditation a priority, bathing me in soothing waves that daily restore my nervous system.

The blessings that flow from the company of holy people are incomparable to any other blessings. Even the love and affection that the gods and the angels possess are nothing compared to the limitless love that flows from the holy ones. It is the characteristic of these enlightened ones to raise others to their own level.

— Yoga Vasistha

Mother Meera, an avatar
who lives in Germany.

Karunamayi, an incarnation
of the Goddess of Wisdom, Saraswati.

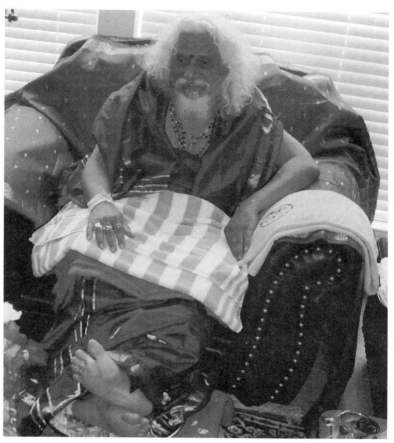

Viswamji Viswawaguru, an incarnation of Dattatreya.

CHAPTER 1

A Wave of Silence:
The Presence of a Saint

"All the Catholic saints are dead. I can't believe you've come all the way to Baton Rouge to see a saint who's alive." Her Louisiana accent carried the words like a gentle breeze. My hostess looked upward, then sideways as she reached theological resolution. "I guess that's the difference between Hinduism and Catholicism," she said.

I had never met Swamiji. A woman in a purple *sari* at a gathering for Ammachi, another great Hindu saint, had introduced me to him through a photograph. Swamiji's dark, piercing eyes, framed by a red turban, stared out at me; he had jet-black hair and a full beard. The *guru's* intensity and power captured my attention. His lips were full, his face youthful and radiant.

I took the picture from her and continued staring at him. Swamiji's intent look had inspired me to make the eight-hour drive from Austin to meet him. I knew nothing about him except that he lived in India and was making a visit to Baton Rouge. But I felt drawn to him. At this time in my life I was ready for a saint, and especially now, after a chaotic siege with a broken foot, which had gone undiagnosed for a month.

The doctor had warned me that I needed surgery, but then might never walk again if I had it. Insurance companies and my employer balked. I felt enraged and vulnerable. After agonizing too long, I finally called the operating room and said I would not show up for the operation scheduled the next morning.

In recompense for my troubles, I was led not to one, but two Indian saints on the same day: Swamiji in Louisiana in the morning and Karunamayi in Texas in the evening. I had seen the lovely saint Karunamayi before. Between the full moon ceremonies honoring the unbroken feet of each of these two great gurus lay a mere seven-hour drive.

Darshan is an audience with and blessing of a holy person. The delicious, brief taste of enlightenment experienced in the presence of a saint—receiving *darshan,* as it is called—was becoming familiar to me, and I pursued it with relish. I found it inspired my perseverance on the spiritual path.

The outwardly non-descript Indian temple in Baton Rouge was smack in the midst of an industrial complex off the main road. Except for the sea of shoes in front, the single storey temple was indistinguishable from the surrounding pale brick buildings. As I approached the entrance I saw bright-colored, swirling chalk designs on the sidewalk. The details of the design, created in honor of Swamiji, left no lasting image, but the feeling was unmistakably Indian. Its intricate swirls and spirals were reminiscent of the long journey back to the Self in the quest for enlightenment. The colored dust residue, which would vanish with the next rain, bespoke the transience of the world and the fleeting chance to enjoy the blessing of Swamiji's rare visit from India. Inside, the distinctly Indian bronze Hindu deities belied the simple exterior of the building. They stood on a low stage at one end of the beige-carpeted room. The jolly, elephant-headed god Ganesh sat with his enormous belly that holds the universe. At his side was his ever-present steed, a scurrying mouse, representing the scattered mind upon which sits the vastness of unindividuated consciousness. Another bronze statue showed Dattatreya, the handsome, three-headed composite of Brahma the Creator of the universe, Vishnu the Sustainer, and Shiva the Destroyer.

Sri Ganapati Sachchidananda Swamiji, an incarnation of this tripartite deity Dattatreya, appeared draped in soft orange sherbet-colored robes. With his slow-moving eyes and lustrous black hair, Swamiji formed an image of unruffled wholeness. He glided to the center of the stage. I sat in the front row seat on the floor with an enormous cast on my left leg jutting out in front of me. I felt the audience stir. Everyone stood up, folded their hands, and bowed their heads.

A wave of calm silence washed over me as he approached a red-cushioned chair surrounded by vases of pale roses. My eyes fixed on his face. As he lowered himself into the large, ornately carved gold chair just inches from me, my eyelids closed, coordinated with his slow downward movement. In the ensuing darkness, I could feel my massive conceptual scaffolding around the dichotomies of right and wrong, acceptable and unacceptable, beautiful and ugly, dissolve into a unitary liquid ocean. The silent wholeness in that moment left no room for anything else. This was a new feeling and it surprised me.

During the introductions, my usual habit of judgment dropped away. It was replaced by a sense of union and appreciation, such as one experiences in nature. The perpetual chatter of my mind slowed and then abruptly stopped. It was not just that my mind and thoughts had settled down, there simply were no thoughts scratching or grasping to achieve some goal. In that moment, the purpose of any possible thought I could construe was fulfilled. With the absence of thoughts came an absence of emotions reacting to them. Missing were the familiar reactive static and oscillating flutter of individuated feelings.

My eyes involuntarily squeezed tight. A waterfall of golden light shot in through the top of my head and drenched my being. My breath stopped. When the infusion ended, I exhaled in a slow, sighing stream that seemed endless. I knew I was in the presence of Divinity.

From my deep peace, I sensed that there was no tension in any cell of Swamiji's body. He moved like softened butter when crossing his legs into the lotus position. As graceful as a lion in slow motion, he lit candles and moved silver-filigreed objects through the air while performing a precise *Vedic* ritual. The wafting scent of burning camphor during this *puja* sent me to a place of ancient remembering and yearning for the sacred.

My wave of tranquility was one of the boons of being in the presence of a master and receiving his *darshan*, his transmission of spiritual energy. And although I had been practicing meditation for many years, the depth of this experience of such flawless silence was new to me.

Unfortunately, I have never been physically near my first and foremost teacher, Maharishi Mahesh Yogi. However, others who have been with him relate remarkable stories about his powerful presence. Maharishi taught me that enlightenment is "the byproduct of a nervous system free of stress." The feeling of wholeness experienced in the presence of such a nervous system seems to be a litmus test for sainthood. The taste of that enlightenment gives one determination to surmount all obstacles to spiritual awakening.

The dynamics, I later learned, are that a realized master is "living fullness" (*poorna*) and his fullness (or *poorna tattva)* spills over onto one in whom it is absent. Nature is also *poorna tattva* and her overflow, likewise creates a feeling of peacefulness in individuals. In the presence of a realized being, there is a wave of tranquility—one feels speechless, at peace.

This profound experience and the yearning to live it again is what drives some devotees to give up their job, give up their home, give all for the sake of enlightenment and a teacher who shows the way. Such behavior may be incomprehensible to those who have never savored an enlightened being's exquisite presence. And, sure enough, some months later, I found that this same engine had intercalated itself into the interstices of my being to drive this behavior in me as well.

When I entered the temple, I followed the example of the mostly Indian participants and "sponsored" the *puja* ritual. As the *Sanskrit* chanting ended, we sponsors moved forward to touch Swamiji's sandals. Touching the feet of a saint is said to destroy all sins and confer immeasurable benefits. The value of touching the sandals is that one receives blessings without the saint having to take on the devotee's *karma*, which would occur if the actual feet were touched. Swamiji sat back at a distance with watchful gaze. Because of my first row position, I was the first to approach and had no model for proper procedure. Acting on instinct, I knelt awkwardly with my cast sticking straight out to the side, put my head to the stage floor, and touched my third eye to his sandal. I noticed, however, that the other devotees walked briskly, bent quickly, barely brushing the sandals with their fingertips as they swept past.

Sitting in a near swoon afterwards, I wondered if my breach of *puja* etiquette was as blatant as putting an elbow in my soup. However, not to worry. Years later, I read that Tibetan Buddhists use their foreheads to touch religious books, statues of deities, or even garments worn by *lamas* they revere. By doing so, they demonstrate their veneration, and also bless themselves with the object touched. So maybe I was not as far off as I had thought.

After the *puja*, an attendant handed each sponsor a silver-colored medal with interlocking geometric designs. The visual pattern formed a *yantra*. It resembles a meditation mantra in that it carries the same kind of concentrated vibrational power.

Swamiji was speaking: "Too much *karmic* debt, like too much sweet, is not good. When you eat too much sweet, you are feeling sick. So, also, with too much *karma*. Too much *karma*, you are feeling bad. So, you must be very, very careful in your actions. You must choose carefully. You must do spiritual practice daily. Please, finish the game. Otherwise, this lifetime just preparation for next lifetime."

Swamiji turned to play an adjacent electric synthesizer. This was as unexpected as Christ picking up an electric guitar. Sheer joy quickly superseded the feeling of incongruity as his music rang through the air. The two great loves of my life, spirituality and music, merged in this moment of innocence, catching me totally off-guard. Swamiji played and sang in a language I did not understand—perhaps Hindi. The beauty of the music was unexpected, and add to that Swamiji's powerful presence, I was in ecstasy. It was divine music, and Swamiji was creating it. Together they vaporized all the internal edges of my mind. From Maharishi I had learned the power of Vedic sounds to heal and to refine the nervous system. Some people have reported dramatic physical healing from Swamiji's music just by listening to his CD's and cassettes. Swamiji's sounds have the refined subtlety of classical music, but his music is neither classical nor traditionally Indian. A visitor from some celestial realm, his music wrapped around my being and transported me to its homeland.

Sitting on the floor to Swamiji's left was a drum player with two *tabla* drums in front of him. His fingers accelerated on the leather until they were a visual blur, creating a distinctly Indian rhythm. His speed quickened to a frenzy, which matched the growing intensity of Swamiji's soulful voice.

The *tabla* player commanded my total attention for a few minutes as I stared at his finger movements and was mesmerized. I imagined how such manual dexterity would translate into sensual pleasure.

As I was having this unabashed and prolonged erotic fantasy, I sensed that Swamiji was thinking, "I like this honest woman." Some moments later, I felt his attention on me again and sensed him thinking, "She has abundant *poorvapoonya* (past life credit). Many people will come to me through her." I felt that Swamiji knew me, knew what I was thinking, and liked me. The absence of barriers enjoyed with a close friend characterized this encounter. In friendship, the development of trust precedes the letting down of one's guard and dancing in the freedom of being fully authentic. With Swamiji, I had made no choice to remove protective barriers. He simply by-passed them. The result was the same —I felt free in being myself, fantasies and all.

The inner silence was still with me when I left the prayer hall for the lunch break. I promptly went to my car and sped to a gas station, possessed with a sudden urgency to have my car checked. The serviceman carefully looked over my Honda. "There's no way you would have made it back to Austin with the car in that condition," he said. I felt relief as I envisioned my paralyzed car in the dreaded Houston deathtrap with furious drivers zooming by on both sides. I waited as he made the repairs.

I wondered if Swamiji's grace had prompted my sudden and uncharacteristic behavior in having the car checked. Further, it appeared he had managed it without my having to forfeit my front row seat.

I was two hours late for the afternoon session, but Swamiji arrived at the packed hall at the same time. He walked down an aisle between the throngs of cross-legged people on the floor. Before the aisle vanished, an attendant walked me through it to the stage. Again I sat, literally, at Swamiji's feet.

His aura once again bathed me in a silence that usurped every space in my mind. It continued to do so all day and all night. This stillness when I was near Swamiji was becoming a recurring ritual.

I returned the next day eager not to break the deep inner quiet by talking. This was an auspicious day—*Guru Poornima*. On this full moon day in July, devotees in India go all out to honor their gurus.

A sea of people dressed in red, purple, and yellow silks filled the prayer hall. We sat on the floor before plates with red rose petals, small mounds of ivory rice kernels, bright red-orange *kum kum* powder, a few blades of long grass, and mustard-colored turmeric. (Hindus use *kum kum* powder to mark the third eye spot on the forehead.)

Swamiji sat silent on the large elevated chair. His mission is to find the souls who were with him in previous lifetimes. His mother, who was his guru, gave him a mantra specifically to use when he "crossed the great waters." This facilitates his finding his former students in other countries so he can continue guiding them to enlightenment. I believe that he was my teacher before. A longtime devotee once explained to me that if one is not destined to be with Swamiji through past association, no meeting will occur.

Radhakrishna, a chubby Hindu priest, walked to the microphone. "We will now have *Pada Puja*, the traditional ceremony to honor the feet of the *guru*," he said. "I talked to Swamiji's devotees in India this morning. They were very sad that Swamiji was not with them for *Guru Poornima*. Around the world today, devotees are worshiping

Swamiji's sandals or pictures of his feet. But you in Baton Rouge are very blessed and lucky to have Swamiji with you in person. You can worship the actual divine feet of His Holiness, our beloved Swamiji."

I used to bristle when I was with a group of Westerners who bowed down to the feet of a man proclaiming himself enlightened. With Swamiji, however, I truly felt I was in the presence of Divinity. The wave of silence and peace, which had descended on me in his presence, gave me certainty. It had not "convinced" me, because in Swamiji's presence I was beyond the mind, in a state of pure feeling—in a state of union without crevices that could harbor thoughts.

The saris of hundreds of devotees sitting on the floor turned the large room into a canvas covered with daubs of multi-colored paint. The white paper plates dotted with colored *puja* ingredients reflected the room as a whole.

With thumbs and forefingers, devotees made offerings of rice. I picked up a few grains of rice with the chanting of each Sanskrit phrase, joining the *puja* that was underway. Eleven o'clock that morning was my designated departure time from Baton Rouge to get to Houston to see the other great Indian saint, Karunamayi.

I felt torn between wanting to show Swamiji proper respect and not wanting to be stuck in rush hour traffic and possibly miss Karunamayi. Breaking etiquette once again—this time more seriously—I stood abruptly while the *puja* was still in progress. The large cast on my leg made getting up from the floor difficult, and I wrenched my back as I twisted upwards to standing. With my cast, Western dress, height, and less-than-graceful rise from the floor, I was hardly inconspicuous. I must have emerged like some strange sea monster from the ocean of people. Like lily pads, merciful, perfectly-spaced openings appeared, big enough for my feet as I exited.

I was sure that Swamiji understood my leaving in the middle of the *puja* even if I did scandalize the Indians in the audience. Only mildly mortified, I made it to the door and out the building, ready to race to Houston. Half-submerged trees rose from glassy swamps along the Louisiana highway. The image formed a suitably mystical environment for transitioning from one saint to the next.

CHAPTER 2

Karunamayi's Grace

arunamayi is the incarnation of Goddess Saraswati.
She says this will be the last lifetime for those who repeat the mantra
"Om Ayim Srim Hrim Saraswati Devyai Namah," a homage to
this Hindu goddess of wisdom.

The cool metal of the tan folding chair supporting me at the Indian Cultural Center in Houston felt luxurious after the cramped, cross-legged floor-sitting in Louisiana. My brain continued its whirring movements from five hours of driving to reach Houston before the rush hour madness. I meditated while waiting for events to begin, blessed again with a front row seat.

A palpable softness soon infused the air, and I sensed Karunamayi's healing presence even before she entered the room. About five minutes later, the diminutive saint, dressed in a red sari, appeared at the back of the hall. Although she is only about five feet tall, her huge aura—felt as a wave of refined light and loving protection—was tangible several feet from her. Karunamayi is said to be the incarnation of Saraswati, the Hindu goddess who is the bestower of knowledge, both spiritual and secular.

Devotees of all ages and dress, from grandmothers to youths, from blue jeans to saris, scrunched toward the aisle when Karunamayi approached. She lingered, touching each person's forehead or hands as she made her way toward the front of the hall. She looked each person in the eye to form a bridge through which her warmth flowed. She repeated this process with everyone in the room, moving through the hall in an inversion of a slow departure.

Once at the front of the room she sat down on an elevated, throne-like chair which dwarfed her small stature. Its ornateness contrasted with her gentle humility. There was nothing angular or harsh in her being. She radiated unadulterated love, without judgment or demands—the kind of undiluted love that must spring from the divine.

At twenty-one, Karunamayi severed ties with home comforts and went to live in the forest. Alone there but for the animals, she meditated and practiced austerities to uplift the world. Twelve years later, she reached God Realization. Soon Karunamayi perceived that her overseas "children" were calling for her. This prompted her to first visit the United States in 1995.

Karunamayi sat in silent observation. Indian vocal music filled the air, and a clinking performance of Indian classical dance ensued. A dancer appeared on stage in sumptuous gold and red silks, her hair pulled back severely, large earrings accenting her prominent dark eyes. A small gold ring circled one of her toes. Tiny bells on her ankles rang with the downward accent of her bare feet slapping the wooden floor to the rhythm of the music. Karunamayi looked on with motherly love at this performance in her honor.

She applauded when the dance ended, then she began to speak, her soft voice almost inaudible. Even with the microphone just inches from her delicate, rounded face, her voice did not carry beyond the first few rows. I was grateful to be sitting close enough to hear her inspiring and gentle words. I basked my ailing body in her light. My stomach was ballooning and my back ached from wrenching it when I had stood up so suddenly to leave Swamiji's *puja*.

"So, children, you must remember to meditate. Only through meditation can we burn our actions." She elaborated on the Saraswati mantra, *Om Ayim Srim Hrim Saraswati Devyai Namah* and its four seed syllables. "The first one, *Om,* is the Supreme Consciousness. It is like a jewel at the beginning of the mantra, and it gives the happiness of supreme bliss. The second syllable *Ayim* dispels the darkness of ignorance and gets rid of *tamasic,* or indolent, tendencies. Chanting *Ayim* keeps negative thoughts from disturbing the mind. *Ayim* is the prime seed syllable for all sound. The next, *Srim,* light, increases awareness. *Hrim* is energy. In the combination of all these syllables, the mantra becomes very powerful. When we say the Saraswati mantra, *Om Ayim Srim Hrim Saraswati Devyai Namah* just one time, it is equal to repeating one thousand names of God. When you repeat the mantra, have in mind that you must not open your eyes. So, with much motherly love I am asking you to let your mind turn inward, and let your meditation be with true devotion and dedication."

After Karunamayi spoke, the audience began singing *bhajans,* Indian devotional hymns. During an *arati* ceremony honoring her, the lights in the hall dimmed. Flames from brass oil lamps moving in slow circles in front of Karunamayi provided the only illumination in the room. Sanskrit chanting echoed while devotees approached her and placed layer after layer of flower garlands on the tiny saint until she seemed in danger of toppling from the weight of them.

Karunamayi moved to the side of the stage as the music subsided. Attendants holding large cardboard boxes of oranges stood beside her. She invited us to come up to receive her blessing and a piece of fruit. The disciple accepts as most precious whatever the guru gives, which is called *prasad.* We knelt to touch her feet.

When I approached, I towered about a foot above her. Although I was looking down with my head, I looked up in reverence with my heart. Karunamayi stretched out her arm and placed her hand on my forehead. In her sweet, soft voice she said,

"Will you be my baby?"

Befuddled by the plethora of gurus and teachers in my life—Maharishi Mahesh Yogi, Ammachi, Swamiji, and now Karunamayi—I simply dodged the question altogether.

"Thank you," I said with non-committal courtesy.

I feared saying yes would bind me in a committed relationship as a disciple. I proceeded to honor Karunamayi by kneeling and then touching her feet on this *Guru Poornima* day, designated most auspicious for honoring gurus. During my second *Pada Puja* ceremony in one day, doubly blessed I touched the feet of a another great saint.

I am not seeking a guru, I reasoned on my way back to my seat, nor the exclusivity that comes with such a relationship. I was already committed, not to a person but to a technique—to Transcendental Meditation.

I had learned it twenty-five years earlier, and that is when the enlightenment bug hit me hard. A poster on campus in the 1970s had touted "Increased Creativity" when one did meditation. "Nonsense. That's impossible. This is hype," I said, and promptly forgot about it. Later when a friend in medical school said he was coming to spend the night, I was anticipating an erratic med student, frazzled from being up most nights. Instead, an integrated, calm man appeared. When I interrogated him about his impossibly calm demeanor given his stressful life, he told me that he practiced Transcendental Meditation (TM). I started right away and saw Maharishi Mahesh Yogi on video during the introductory course and later on retreats.

To Maharishi, my first guru, I am ever grateful for this daily meditation practice, which has been the mainstay of my life for the past many years. I attribute to TM both my initial spiritual awakening and my continuous growth on the spiritual path.

Along with the Vedic knowledge Maharishi brought out for the world, he taught me that to be in tune with nature is to be in tune with the will of God.

What I was not able to receive from Maharishi, because of the enormity of his worldwide following, was personal contact with him.

He has stated that he is not a personal guru. He has structured his movement to create many teachers whereby he can replicate his capacity to pass on the sacred knowledge of India. My seeking out Indian saints is not a reflection of dissatisfaction with any of Maharishi's teachings, which I hold precious. Rather, it reflects my yearning for the joy that comes from being in the presence of a divine soul, a joy I seek frequently.

—❈—

Some people, of course, did not understand. "You're just a guru-chaser," my sister accused me once. Although I denied it vehemently, it was true that I had driven the five hours from Austin to Dallas just two weeks before to see Ammachi, the Indian saint who hugs. Maybe I was a guru-chaser, I retorted to myself, but that was better than many other more unsavory pursuits. After all, the precepts of many religions say to "be in the company of holy people."

The yearning for illumination had grown each subsequent year to eclipse everything else in my life. What I could not easily relate to gaining enlightenment I deemed either irrelevant or a necessary nuisance. In visiting saints, I was seeking to bask in their light to boost me on my spiritual path.

While devotees ate a midnight vegetarian feast, I left the building anxious to begin the three-and-a-half hour drive before me. On leaving, I clashed head-on with the real world. I was in some altered state— my mind was simultaneously expanded from the *darshan* (grace) of saints and brain-fried from too many hours of driving already. I felt distinctly incompetent to pilot my car back home. The situation worsened dramatically as I left the quiet residential area and drove onto the four-lane highway in Houston. My capacity to make sense of visual cues disintegrated; the discrete bits of information dissolved into a boundless blur. I jumped from a state of feeling protected among the holy to a state of holy terror. For the next thirty minutes I drove through Houston in stark terror, my elbows hunched toward my head like a *rigor mortised* chicken.

Cars zoomed in front of me and behind me, pushing me up to their 80-mile-an-hour speed. Then they channeled my car, at a speed I could not endure, into a single lane with concrete barriers extending for miles and miles on both sides. They threatened to splat me at any moment and refused to disappear as the speed increased. I kept repeating, "Jesus Christ is driving this car. Jesus Christ is driving this car." It helped me endure, but it did not calm my fears. Finally, the buildings began thinning out, as did the cars and their distance from me. My heart rate normalized.

The physical discomfort and emotional upheaval during driving seemed antithetical to the beatific experience I had anticipated would be the afterglow of my Herculean effort to obtain saints' blessings. Perhaps the stomach and back pain I had experienced in Karunamayi's presence was more purification before a spiritual growth spurt. In any case, I did enjoy the satisfaction of pulling off two *darshan* events in the same day, each separated by a state line and 300 miles.

I drove wearily the rest of the three and a half hours home to Austin. At four A.M. I drove up and down the green hills, leading to Radiance, my precious meditation community in Austin. Kindred, inward-directed souls pursuing spiritual evolution dwelled here. All the houses were dark. Three deer grazed safe in the shadows in a yard near my house. My mega-mile, mega-guru day had ended.

CHAPTER 3

Call to India

Just as a candle cannot burn without fire,
men cannot live without a spiritual life.

— Buddha

Back at home, the wafting smell of burning camphor from Swamiji's
puja kept returning to haunt me. Its pungent smell was in my hair and
did not dissipate, even with regular washing. A souvenir book of Swamiji
photographs next to my bed likewise had an enduring fragrance of camphor for weeks. The silver *yantra* medal I received at his *puja* began
turning an unexpected yellowish ochre color. The change reminded me
of miracles associated with apparitions of the Blessed Mother in
Medjugorje, Yugoslavia. Many pilgrims in Medjugorje reported looking down to discover that their rosaries had turned gold.

Was this a message to me? Or was it the product of an overactive
imagination, or perhaps a special additive in the metal designed to sway
the gullible? My musings soon got lost in the rapid pace of a psychologist

25

being back in the work-a-day world. Sadly, so did the silence I had known in Swamiji's presence. The memory of the taste of silence beyond thoughts that distinguished my visit to Swamiji from the other saints was creating a longing to experience it again.

After working with ailing patients all day, I would lie in bed at night reading and again become aware of the subtle smell of camphor. Its nudging reminder carried with it my nagging questions: What was that experience I had of total silence with him in Louisiana? What would it be like to have the mental chatter permanently stopped even while being in the world? Was it even possible?

⚜

A newsletter arrived one day from the temple in Louisiana. It contained information about Swamiji's travels. Out of curiosity, I called the number listed.

"Are people allowed to visit Swamiji in India?" I said.

"With Swamiji's permission it is allowed. The best time to visit is in November when it's cooler."

"Where is the ashram?"

"It's in Mysore"

"And where is Mysore? I mean, what airport do you fly into?"

"All that information we can give you. But first you must get Swamiji's permission."

"Are you in touch with the people at the ashram in India?"

"Yes, I telephone them almost every week," the man said.

"I wonder, then, could you ask for permission for me? There's no rush, but, just some time when you are calling India anyway."

"I can request permission. Swamiji travels a great deal to different countries, so he's not always there in Mysore. When were you thinking of going?"

"Well, I wasn't. I mean, I can't go. I don't have the finances or the time off. I called because I was curious to know if it was even possible to see him. It's unlikely, though, that I will actually make the trip."

I recognized this push-pull movement within me—much like the shaking of a rocket before takeoff: it was the forerunner of travel.

Maps and pictures of other cultures and countries had always drawn me like a magnet. As a chubby five-year-old, I would stand on my bed stretching to point with pudgy fingers to capitals of different countries on the map over my bed. I engaged in this nightly ritual while my mother sat on the edge of the bed gazing lovingly at me. Now, as an adult, I still love to pour over travel brochures and to find creative ways to travel on a low budget. However, given my usual five-day jaunts with modest airfares, India was in an entirely different league.

Several weeks passed without a call. By then I had let go of the idea of India and was unconcerned.

CHAPTER 4

Loosening Rigid Barriers

What is Truth? A difficult question; but I have solved it for myself by saying that it is what the "voice within" tells you.
— Mahatma Gandhi

The phone rang one Saturday. It was Rao from the Swamiji center in Mississippi.

"Swamiji has given his blessings for you to go to the ashram," he said.

In the meantime, unexpected income had shifted the boundaries of the impossible. The yearning to go to India, a place with little appeal before now, was becoming overwhelming. What else was there, after all, but the quest for enlightenment? Life is short, and then you die. If not now, when?

Nothing could stop me. No hurdle was too high. Like a homing pigeon driven by sheer instinct, I determined to make my way back to the source of that silence I'd known briefly. I was familiar with inner quiet through meditation. However, the absolute silence without thoughts I had experienced with Swamiji was new and compelling.

I had ordered a videotape of Swamiji performing a fire ceremony and when it arrived, I quickly popped it into the player. As he sat beside a stone fire pit throwing oblations into the flames, his well-oxygenated flesh looked plumped up from within by buoyant circulation, disallowing any wrinkles. Penetrating eyes peered out from above his full, black beard. They never darted, but rather they sailed slowly across the horizon of their orb. The soft rose sari, draped across his body contrasted with jet-black hair and chestnut skin.

Later in this *puja* to honor the elemental force of fire, Swamiji actually stood in the fire pit. His flesh should have been sizzling and his robes on fire, but they were not. The flames shooting up around him did not burn him. Looking transfigured, Swamiji added more oblations to the fire while still standing within it. He bent down, his face merging into the flames, and reached to the base of the fire. With unprotected hands, he pulled a *shiva lingam,* a hand-sized oval stone embodying Shiva, the god who destroys all that binds. Now I wonder if this was a foreshadowing of Nature throwing me into a purificatory fire in India.

These images of Swamiji had a powerful effect on me. I knew I had made the right decision to go to India and became more certain of my wisdom with each viewing of the tape.

I requested an extensive leave of absence from work in a tone so determined that my employer could not refuse it. Then I was free to devote myself fully to that alone which overshadowed all else in importance—the quest for enlightenment. This particular enlightenment catalyst conveniently fulfilled a confluence of yearnings, including my powerful wanderlust.

I discovered a tribe of devotees in different lines of work—Swamiji's unseen hands—who synchronistically made all things possible. One of them, a travel agent in New York, found me a ticket at $3,000 less than the American Airlines fare to India. It included stopovers to visit Mother Meera, an Indian saint in Germany, and to visit family in Washington, D.C. for Christmas on the way back.

In 1994, a friend gave me a photograph of Mother Meera for Christmas. It sat on a shelf near my bed, and from it her penetrating eyes peered out at me and seemed to plumb the depths of my soul. My curiosity awakened, I borrowed a book about her and learned that she transmits spiritual energy through her photograph and receives visitors from around the world who schedule meetings with her in Germany.

Moved by her photograph and the book, I yearned to see her in person. Along with four friends, I arranged a trip to Germany, despite the fact that I was in tight financial straits. Between making the plans and the actual trip, my house caught fire while I was at work. It was a blessed, self-extinguishing fire. The electrical element in the water heater burst into flames setting the attic on fire. This caused the water in the tank to heat up, blowing a gasket, and spewing out water which extinguished the fire. I reported the blaze to the Fire Department who was about to dispatch trucks. "That won't be necessary," I said and explained that the fire had extinguished itself. "Ma'am, we don't get many fires like that," the operator said in a Texas drawl.

The damage to the attic was, nonetheless, extensive. The insurance company insisted that during the repairs I live in a hotel for two weeks, just at the time I planned to be in Germany. They happily picked up the hotel tab for my entire stay in Germany, eliminating the financial stress associated with the trip. The insurance company adjuster even commented that the hotel in Germany was very reasonable. Was this divine intervention? Certainly, something unusual.

My meeting with Mother Meera was quietly satisfying. During the silent meetings with her over eight days, I felt cleansed and cloaked with divine protection. Mother Meera is an Indian *avatar*, a divine incarnation who comes to benefit humanity. She lives in a small town in Germany near Limburg. Thousands come to see her and to receive her silent blessing. Mother Meera gives *darshan* in total silence for four consecutive days each week. Devotees kneel before her. She holds devotees' heads for a few minutes and performs a delicate procedure whereby she untangles any knots in channels along the spine and removes obstacles to spiritual practice.

Two white lines seen only by certain enlightened beings start at the toes and go up along the legs. At the base of the spine, they join, forming a single line to the top of the head. The lines are thinner than a hair, and if they are broken, a person's life is in danger. When Mother touches a devotee's head, a light moves up the line like a meter, indicating the development of one's spiritual practice. If spiritual aspiration weakens, the line moves downward. If the white lines reach the top of the head, the Supreme Self will have revealed itself to the devotee. If the lines reach above the head, the devotee will be in constant contact with the divine.

In the front of the body are two red lines going upward on either side of the legs. If the red lines reach the white lines at the base of the spine, the person will have achieved absolute detachment. After untying knots, Mother Meera looks silently into the devotee's eyes to detect any problem areas in the person's life to which she can direct her energy and healing light. In giving Light she opens every part of a person's being to that Light.

Over subsequent years I have been blessed to return to Germany three times to see Mother Meera. Since that first meeting with her in 1995, when the inner yearning was clear and strong, I have jumped at every opportunity to see living saints. This was the beginning of my saint-hopping hegiras.

⊰⊱

In preparation for my journey to India, I visited a "travel clinic" located in a bustling medical complex. Colorful posters of exotic places adorned the walls. One wall, plastered with postcards from travelers, attested to the survival-enhancing benefits of their visit to the clinic. From a crisply dressed nurse whose face radiated years of healthy eating choices, I learned that dengue fever is a killer carried by mosquitoes and is prevalent in India.

"And currently there's an epidemic of malaria. It's a new strain that kills its victims in a week," she mused cheerfully. I learned that flying mosquito monsters victimize the unwary between dawn and dusk. She recommended a particularly noxious repellant to be used at all times along with long-sleeved shirts.

"The repellent causes some neurological damage, but it is better than getting malaria.

"Don't pet any cats or dogs, or go near wild animals. They don't inoculate pets, so rabies is rampant. Should you accidentally be scratched by a cat, go immediately to a hospital and seek treatment.

"All water throughout India is considered contaminated. Don't even trust regular bottled water because people often refill containers with tap water and sell them. The only safe choice is carbonated water. Bring powdered Gatorade to replace electrolytes and to avoid dehydration during bouts of dysentery. Should you become ill, you could easily lose several liters of fluid in a day.

"No dairy. No raw vegetables. Don't eat fruit unless it comes with a protective carapace. People use beaches and riverbanks as toilets. Parasites carpet them and burrow up through the feet to the brain. Only walk on beaches with rubber shoes. We do *not* recommend swimming. Should you feel compelled to go into the Ganges, immediately dry off with a towel and douse yourself from head to foot with alcohol. Carry your own syringes in case you have to go to the hospital. Sometimes they re-use syringes on different people. And be observant about what goes into the syringe. One of our patients got very sick because they injected him with white shoe polish. They put it in the syringe because it looked like the white penicillin they had run out of."

By the end of her spiel, I was terrified, my horror quelled only slightly by my punctures from immunizing shots against the host of tropical diseases. I left the clinic frazzled yet no less determined to reach my destination in India. I hauled hefty supplies of malaria pills and antiseptic toilettes for washing my hands, my eating utensils, and the rims of drinking glasses. I had enough diarrhea medicine to treat a herd of elephants and an oral vaccine containing live typhoid bacteria to put on ice like caviar and to take in subsequent days to prevent the disease.

It was a sobering, if not terrifying visit. It provided yet another opportunity to balance the two extremes of the control continuum:

personal responsibility for well-considered choices at one end, and at the other end, turning everything over to God.

I caught a glimpse of my faintly furrowed brow surrounded by wild curly locks in the bathroom mirror. My image gave the dilemma concrete visual form: the spirit made flesh. For these were precisely the kinds of situations that pitted my soaring spirit against my discriminating mind, which, like a knife dicing the onion of the universe, busied itself chopping, dividing, and dissecting everything. The mind-chatter cooked up a soup of irresolvables: should I have trusted in God and foregone the travel clinic? Going to a travel clinic as a prelude to a spiritual pilgrimage for guarantees against illness was the antithesis of trust. An Indian renunciate forsaking all for God, wandering half-clothed with only a begging bowl does not go to a travel clinic first, I mused.

Then again, perhaps there was no violation of trust in God. Perhaps the option of the travel clinic was just a demonstration of God's grace and mercy. Through God's grace, I could afford to go to a travel clinic. God blessed me with living in the West and having access to medical research. It delineated for me the various horrors potentially awaiting me in the tropics of India and secured their prevention. Later in India, however, this seeming resolution of my soup of conflicts began to unravel.

CHAPTER 5

Faith vs. Control

*Faith is not something to grasp,
it is a state to grow into.*

— Mahatma Gandhi

Another opportunity for faith vs. control arose just days before my scheduled departure: my visa had not arrived. My passport, which was to be stamped with my visa, was also at large in the universe. I had trustingly sent it off to the Indian embassy. As the clock ticked closer to my departure date, I left many urgent, unanswered phone messages at the consulate. An answering machine, rather than a real person, always received my pleas.

Should I be proactive or trusting? Was this a test? Was it an opportunity to demonstrate an unwavering, calm mind, and surrender to God's will (which might not include a trip to India)? Maharishi, my first and foremost teacher, often said, "Take it as it comes. But if it doesn't come, go get it."

34

Perhaps I had blithely sent my passport into oblivion. After bouts of trusting and letting go, I reverted to control mode. I made another round of numerous phone inquiries, this time about the logistics of getting a new passport. I made calls to the travel agent. And, bypassing the regional office in Houston, I called the national Indian embassy in Washington instead, where more answering machines awaited me.

Rao was my contact person at the Swamiji Center in Mississippi. In this journey of crossing the waters, he was my Indian link to safety. He soothed me with his deep resonant voice. As Swamiji's long-term devotee, he represented a rivulet of the ocean of silence that Swamiji embodied. Rao's voice echoed the silence I knew and for which I thirsted.

"I'll see what I can do," he said after I described my passport woes.

Something about the silence in his voice made me trust that he would resolve the problem even though he was in Mississippi, far from the Houston embassy that had captured my passport.

Cooking with time pressures on all fronts, I scurried about, my wild brown hair streaming behind me. I finished up dwindling-but-still-powerful mountains of paperwork. I wrote out my will and sought closure on a variety of unfinished, often insignificant tasks, which suddenly took on urgency far beyond their merit.

As my work ended and my six-month leave of absence began, I mulled over how difficult my work for the nursing home had been. Hour after hour, week after week, I shared the pain of illness and the loneliness of abandonment and impending death. I could feel tears begin to well up and run down my cheeks as I thought of how much time I spent being with others in their pain, and then felt troubled and hurt that I so quickly burned out others when I was in need.

I lowered my head into the pillow and cried as images of thousands of patients whose pain I had shared flooded my mind. They were souls whose bodies and minds had already half-abandoned them as their frail bones lay curled in nursing home beds. I remembered feeling horribly humbled by my limited ability to help.

Not knowing what else to do I once offered to say a prayer, only to hear,

"Yes, please say a prayer. Hold my hand and say it out loud so I can hear. Tell God to let me die.

At such times, I reached the edge of my resources, my boundaries, my training. What clever tools could I pull from my bag of psychology tricks? What textbook theory or training to halt suicidal behavior could meet head-on the screeching reality of a patient's cry which was based on such a clear, accurate assessment of reality? For it was true that the patient's body was no longer able to meet the basic demands of living without agonizing pain. The future held nothing more promising than another day within the walls of a nursing home. The high point of the day was someone answering a call bell before nature took its course all over the sheets.

I remembered the many times I would circle the nursing home in my car, trying to forestall even for a few moments, the descent into the living inferno of suffering to which I had become both accomplice and witness. I tried, often futilely, to lessen the pain of the succession of souls in misery who comprised my days. I cried for them, and I cried for myself. I had tried.

Often the price I paid was having nothing left for the rest of my day, no energy for the lighter things. Human contact became a threat, another occasion for the neediness of others to suck me dry. It led to a kind of isolation, a de-normalization of life where my only human contact was a foray into profound misery.

Over the previous ten years, I sat with hundreds of patients whose cruel clash with destiny via a ten-second car crash upended their lives. These patients are permanently unknown to the eager New Age healers preferring to lay hands on the well—the unhospitalized, uncrippled, worried, baby-boomers, obsessing over their next grey hair, their sagging bosom or erectile dysfunction.

This rerun of my painful work was the temporary closing of a long chapter and the transition to a new adventure in consciousness growth in India.

—※—

Two days before my scheduled departure date, Rao called back.

"It's all been taken care of. You'll have your passport tomorrow morning."

"You're a miracle worker!" I said. "How did you do it?"

Calmly, competently he said, "I called the ambassador."

The details hung in the cavern of the imagination.

CHAPTER 6

Feasting on Sanctity: Pilgrimage to India

The value of a pilgrimage is in setting aside our familiar worldly concerns to focus on God, in loosening the rigid barriers that separate us from the divine.

I was open to the idea of taking a pilgrimage of my own because I had already enjoyed a modern version in the form of meditation retreats in the U.S. To Maharishi I give thanks for these respites lasting for days or months. They cleanse stress from the nervous system more powerfully than anything else I have experienced. He has structured in-residence "courses" to free participants from all other responsibilities, including meal preparation and dealing with family and business issues. In this removal from one's daily life—freedom from all usual obligations—the nervous system is able to experience extraordinarily deep rest. From this state of continuing low metabolic rate, low physical activity, and great silence, stresses are released. This leads to profound and refreshing restoration, bringing one closer and closer to the innocence of a child.

—⋈⋊—

Lufthansa, the paragon of order and cleanliness, was the airline transporting me to Bombay, where geography reconfigures familiar rules governing day-to-day living. The plane's sound system alone was worth the flight. Technical precision delivered strains of Mahler symphonies and Chopin nocturnes, soothing my ragged nervous system. The smell of fresh lavender laced the moisturizing lotion in the airplane lavatories. Its application offset the usual feeling of grunginess I have known on transatlantic flights.

Twenty-some hours later I arrived in India, weary but eager. Another flight from Bombay to Bangalore awaited me.

A midnight bus transferred me across town from the international to the national airport. The time of reckoning had begun. An expanse of wetness on the floor assaulted my senses during my first foray into the airport bathroom. Then, exiting to the waiting room for check-in, I had my first inkling that chairs were a thing of the past. I joined others squatting awkwardly on luggage carts to wait.

A few hours later, I boarded a surprisingly elegant flight to Bangalore. Sitting on a crimson velvet seat, I enjoyed an exotic meal replete with linen napkins, and did not even consider that they might harbor parasite number one.

At the Bangalore airport, the luggage dropping onto the conveyor belt told of different times, different cultures. There was a preponderance of large, travel-worn boxes. With determined intent, the senders tied them using multiple wrappings of string or sheets of plastic.

I followed directions to secure a pre-paid taxi in the airport to avoid overpaying. The taxi sign above the bare counter with three clerks leaning on it was the only mark of officialdom. The attendant stared unabashedly at the contents of my wallet as I secured the fee. Perhaps based on what he observed, he added a contrived "service charge."

It was four hours to the ashram. The taxi shared the road with sacred cows; with slate-colored, hunch-backed oxen tiredly hauling their loads; with bicycles impossibly loaded with mountains of wares—car tires, bales of golden straw, or dozens of green melons with thick, corrugated skins. Bright saris of sumptuous elegance contrasted with beige dirt roads and humble shops and dwellings. Even in the construction pits, women wore colorful saris as they swung huge hammers to crack boulders. Dry, dusty air penetrated the taxicab in sudden gusts. Everywhere the din was deafening. However, the exotic images were an invigorating antidote to the fatigue from two days of travel.

In Mysore, the ashram rose like a mirage. It was a grand, luxurious compound of several buildings, some architecturally exquisite. A larger-than-life-size photograph of Swamiji, with shining ebony hair, beard, and dark eyes, dressed in a rose-colored sari, looked down from high above the entrance gate. Gently swaying palm trees lined broad cobble-stone walkways, wide as avenues. Herb and flower gardens were abundant. Signs in front of them described esoteric links between the plants and different planets. A clay-colored pottery statue of a woman draped in leaves stood as tall as a small building. She was designated as the spirit of herbs and plants, who, when prayed to, alleviates addictions.

A robust soul with a hearty handshake greeted me.
"Welcome to India," he said with an unmistakable, curry-flavored accent and a narrow range of pitches.

"I'm Radhakrishna. You probably want to rest after your long journey. You'll be staying in Angel Hall."

"Angel Hall?" I said. "That's an interesting name."

"Swamiji calls the foreigners 'angels.' He said you all travel so far in airplanes to get here that you are like angels. So when the dorm was built, it was called Angel Hall."

Following Swamiji's example, everyone throughout the ashram referred to foreigners as angels.

I appreciated the mosquito netting around my dormitory bed and the Western bathroom facilities in Angel Hall.

The next morning in the prayer hall my eyes feasted on an ancient, bearded man draped to his feet in orange and hunched over a long stick. The man, in his late seventies, seemed to have been attending to temple duties for decades. His long practice had cultured reverence into his cells. He greeted me and assigned me to a straw mat spread on the stone floor. I obeyed and walked up to it at the front of the room where I sat cross-legged with the other angels. Men sat to the left, women to the right.

Giant tongues of fire were leaping from a stone pit in the platform in front of me. Half-naked men clad in *dhotis* (loin cloths) stood around the flames chanting in Sanskrit. They threw oblations of clarified butter into the fire in observance of some ancient ritual.

Priests chanted around the fire pit for about an hour. Then a curtain parted to reveal Swamiji, sitting cross-legged in profile. Surrounded by burning candles and silver ceremonial objects, he performed a *puja* as if in slow motion. The sacredness was palpable. In the States, I had experienced the wafting scent of Eastern spirituality for only moments at a time. It dissipated with the turning of a page in a book of deep red Tibetan mandalas or with the completion of a yearly *Guru Poorrnima* celebration. Here in the ashram prayer hall, the sanctity was pervasive and enduring. I wept with gratitude for immersion in this form of holiness I had known previously only for brief moments.

We ate breakfast in the vast open courtyard. Spanning one side was a newly constructed music hall with a sweeping roof. An Indian version of the Sydney Opera House, it looked perched for take off. Swamiji designed the open-air structure, an acoustically and aesthetically magnificent building, financed, no doubt, by devotees eager to perpetuate values Swamiji was re-kindling after the diluting influence of invading cultures. Instead of rows of seats, there were stepped stone platforms lined with individual mats. The hall contained portraits of great musicians from around the world.

Our morning meal consisted of cooked grain tinted yellow with turmeric and punctuated by black mustard seeds and other unidentifiable spices. We ashramites lined up with high-rimmed, round steel platters that were twice the size of dinner plates. A stocky Indian stood before a large vat and served the food. His *rudraksha* beads, sacred to Shiva, entwined the hair on his bare chest. Using a shovel-like instrument, he delivered each serving with an energetic splat.

A crowd of about two hundred, holding their laden, glistening, silvery plates, squatted on the ground in the large plaza. Some stood. All ate with their hands, scooping food with well-trained thumbs and forefingers. I joined them, awkwardly putting food into my mouth simultaneously wanting to wipe my hands.

We eight angels stood apart in half-Western, half-Indian dress. Our incomplete attire contrasted with the brightly colored, flowing saris of the Indian women and the more restricted, vertical *dhotis* worn by men. It was early in the day, and the sun was already hot. It shimmered on the sea of stainless steel discs dotting the cobblestone expanse.

CHAPTER 7

Getting Less Than Expected

No appointment, no disappointment.
— *Sri Ganapati Sachchidananda Swamiji*

Swamiji was giving "interviews," a highlight of an ashram stay. I sat cross-legged on the stone floor with fifty or so waiting people and wrote down my questions. Rao had warned that Swamiji's presence is so powerful that thoughts, plans, and questions often dissolve when one is near him. One question was about my *dharma,* or life purpose. As I wrote down the question I wondered whether my *dharma* was to be a teacher of Transcendental Meditation (TM). The line was moving at a fast clip. The interviews only lasted a few minutes. Once in the room with Swamiji I felt in control, and I was determined to stay in control.

"How are you?" Swamiji said.

"I'm very, very happy." This phrase came back to haunt me. It would blend in retrospect with Swamiji's words some days later: "There

43

is no difference between happiness and unhappiness. Happiness is a feeling only."

I launched into my agenda of questions.

"What is my *dharma*?"

"It is what you think," he said.

"Does my extreme tiredness doing health care work mean that I am out of *dharma*? Or is it due to *karma*? Or is it just a natural consequence of service work?"

"This is natural," he said. "This is natural."

"Should I change my career to music?"

"You do some research in that," he said.

He handed me a stone hanging on a red string necklace and dismissed me.

I was disappointed. The scene violated my expectations, and I was irritated that Swamiji reflected everything back for me to answer.

"If I could have figured it out myself, why would I have bothered to ask or even come to India?" I thought.

A sudden flash of insight showed me that I had already written the script of my visit way back in the States and that India was not cooperating. This initial pique was a seed of an incipient inchoate feeling that something in my experience of India was amiss.

—◁▷—

Apart from my irritation, however, I was settling into the ashram quite nicely. I slept well and woke up early to meditate. Before the sun rose, I went to the pyramid-shaped meditation building constructed for exclusive use by angels. An outside fountain at the top of the building sent water flowing down the four sides of the slanted roof. Inside, opalescent marble floors shone in the starkness of the bare meditation room. A large bronze statue of Ganesh, the elephant-headed god of the Indian pantheon, was the only ornament in the beautiful room. Carved sandalwood screens covered the otherwise open windows.

Sunlight from behind outlined the honey-colored carvings depicting peacocks, deer, and nature scenes.

At the apex of the pyramid-shaped ceiling was a six-pointed, star-shaped glass window. The building was designed so that the rays of the sun entered through this skylight at dawn. The sun cast a star-shaped pattern on the person sitting in meditation on the floor below it. The building was unlocked only from 5:30 to 6:30 in the morning and from 5:00 to 6:00 in the evening. In compliance with Swamiji's order, the room was open only when the setting and rising sun created the most auspicious times for meditation.

The beauty and serenity of the room were a just reward for early rising. Besides, it meant a complete turnaround of my usual late-night, late-morning schedule. I was adapting to the new timetable with little resistance. In this regard, my purpose in coming to India seemed to be working. I wanted to undergo whatever internal and external rearrangements of my body and psyche would speed up the inexorable march to enlightenment by a few lifetimes.

The *puja* desk opened each morning before prayers. People could sponsor the day's *yagyas*—Vedic rituals to bring about a desired event or transformation. Each morning, I arranged to have a *yagya* for my rapid enlightenment. Yet, my clear intent to maximize opportunities for enlightenment yielded challenges to which I would not have knowingly agreed. With each morning *yagya,* I naively sent off a request to the universe, never anticipating its fierce response.

CHAPTER 8

More Than I Bargained For

Western illusion: Overcoming the senses is just a matter of turning on a switch. The Indian saints who live in the forest or in snowy mountain caves never struggled. They just flipped a switch or opted not to pay attention to anything uncomfortable. Therefore, they never suffered discomfort.

Correction: This is unrealistic wishful thinking. The overcoming of the senses is not automatic. One attains it in increments.

After two days of restful life at the ashram, two hundred devotees from various part of India were gathering for a *kriya* yoga course conducted by Swamiji. *Kriya* is the regular practice of temple worship. Yoga strengthens the body and nervous system while disciplining the energies of the mind and body. Practitioners learn to regulate the breath and the flow of life force through the nervous system.

To prepare for the course, the angels forayed into Mysore to get the requisite attire. We rode in "auto-rickshaws." These open-air, motorized, three-wheeled taxis are a modern version of the rickshaws previously powered by people. They are less expensive than the regular four-wheeled taxis with closing doors. The open-air design puts passengers at the mercy of exhaust from cars and trucks. However, it also lends immediacy to the Indian streets teeming with ever-colorful mixtures of exotic animals and variously draped people.

Amidst bolts of exquisite silks and while being plied with cups of tea, we selected from a variety of white fabrics with subtly patterned textures. Our fabric selections yielded white *Punjabi* dresses down to the mid-calf, worn with matching loose, white pants gathered at the ankles. We were also to wear white scarves, about two yards in length, covering our chests. Men also wore white, either pants with long shirts, or cloth draped from waist to foot, with bare chests. Ashram staff warned course participants that color was distracting to Swamiji and was strictly prohibited during the course. The shop whipped up our *Punjabi* dresses in a few hours' time and delivered them to the ashram.

The rapid onset of a mysterious sore throat the night before made me wary of going to the course. Its location was a few hours away in relative wilderness. "What if this should develop into dengue fever or some serious malady that requires being airlifted to a doctor back in the States?" I thought. In the morning, however, I decided to trust God and go.

Chartered buses took the group to Swamiji's birthplace, Mekedatu, located about four hours from the ashram. Far from civilization, it rests in a beautiful natural setting at the confluence of three rivers: Kaveri, Arkavati, and Gupta Gamini. The Kaveri River is the Ganges of the South.

But during the three-and-a-half-hour bus ride to Mekedatu, the atmosphere began to change. What had been exotic became unbearable. Each bump along the endlessly rocky, pitted road jammed a piece of steel into the base of my spine from beneath the inadequately padded seat. A sickening smell of black, sooty exhaust from the mélange of loud, diesel-burning vehicles wafted in through the open windows. Deafening, high-pitched Indian vocal music blasted over the loud speakers in our overstuffed bus. This aggravated my now powerful sore throat, which lots of vitamin C and echinacea had not relieved.

All of this exacerbated a growing sense of rejection I felt from Swamiji. That morning at the ashram, Swamiji had seemed to push me away. He seemed irritated and did not answer my question when I asked whether I should do "physiological research in music." Instead, he shooed me away. Turning from me, he began speaking in Telugu to the people behind him. "I didn't come all the way to India to be treated with rudeness," I thought.

The long-awaited release from the bus finally arrived. As I alighted at Mekedatu I noticed with dismay that the red string necklace Swamiji had given me had "melted" across my new white *Punjabi* dress. It left a large red smear extending all the way across my chest.

There were only two narrow buildings at the site, surrounded by wilderness as far as the eye could see. A white building was Swamiji's house. The other, an absurdly tall, skinny building, across from Swamiji's quarters housed permanent staff. It looked like the Escher drawing of a building with endless staircases leading nowhere.

With dread, I learned that we were to sleep outdoors on the ground, in the open air. What about the death-wielding mosquitoes? The course was to be a week long. Some angels, most of them hearty Germans, had brought sleeping bags whereas I had only a light blanket. I was unprepared. The other course participants spread their sleeping mats on the dirt ground with no protection from the open air. The Germans climbed up eight flights of stairs winding around the outside of the tall building to procure spots on the rooftop. I followed them and spread my blanket near a drainpipe on the flat roof and left for the evening meal.

Earlier I had seen a kitchen helper hosing down stainless steel dinner plates that lay on the dirt ground. At dinner, an attendant handed me a plate with (contaminated?) water still on it. By this time, I was coughing up mounds of thick, green mucous. When I got up from dinner I saw something like black shoe polish smeared over a few feet of my white scarf. It was my only scarf, my required uniform for yoga class, and I had wanted it to double as the towel I hadn't brought.

I walked to the evening meeting in the prayer hall. Sitting cross-legged in my tiny assigned spot on the floor was agonizing. Carefully folded individuals surrounded me on all sides. They were mostly Indians with years of practice and flexibility encoded in their genes.

The toilet assaulted my senses. Sopping wet floor and sopping wet toilet seat traumatized me in my ill, germ-phobic state. Yards of my white *Punjabi* suit and scarf fell onto the wet toilet while I tried to avoid sitting. The strong back pain from cross-legged sitting intensified as I leaned forward, my upper torso parallel to the floor. The unbearable pain of my position and the fear of the germ-infested toilet seat trapped me between the equal dangers of Scylla and Charybdis. Unable to withstand the pain anymore, I finally collapsed onto the toilet seat. Drawn in by a rationalization which some wiser, more recessed part of me knew was truth, I felt my being surrender. "It's all God, anyway—the filth, the wetness, everything—and everywhere—the entire expanse of the universe," I thought.

The quintessential experience of India for me was that circumstances repeatedly pulled me to the brink where, grasping onto the edge of the cliff that was my intellect, I finally just had to let go. Each time, the letting go brought me out of the capsule of the head, where I lived so much of my life, into the core of the immediate experience, (in its sometimes disgusting fullness).

Sobered, I trudged up the eight flights of stairs, legs aching, to the sleeping quarters on the roof. It was a beautiful starry night. Eager for the anesthesia and amnesia of sleep, I slid under my blanket and sat, wedged in like a sardine among eight bossy German angels telling me what to do. They were incapable of speaking a sentence without the words "you should." Rock sure, each "you should" sent my way had been preceded by some accommodating gesture on my part. My interactions with them made me feel stretched on a rack. Finally, exhausted, and yearning for sleep I laid my head down onto the concrete into a seething nest of beetles. There were hundreds. Horrified, I made efforts to sweep them away, trying to avoid getting them into the other angels' sleeping spots.

At three-thirty in the morning a short-lived amnesia dissolved. I awoke freezing. I pulled at my unyielding blanket and clothes, trying to stretch them to generate some additional coverage and warmth. When these efforts failed, I drank hot water from my precious thermos. At dawn loud speaker music shot me into wakefulness. I removed a beetle from my underarm. Facing the filthy toilet first thing in the morning was almost more than I could bear. And the flushing mechanism was broken. With yards of white cloth flanking me and without toilet paper, the cleanup afterwards was that of an inexperienced hand. Pain lodged deeply in my body from sitting cross-legged so much and from sleeping on cold concrete. And now I was sneezing great gobs of green slime. "The bacteria are taking over." No tissues, no toilet paper, no stores for necessities to manage the frequent sneezing. A wet washcloth, green and brown from use, was doubling as Kleenex. It was going to be my towel. Then it was going to have to be my toilet paper.

I dragged the weary weight of my body up the eight flights of stairs back to the rooftop to sit and meditate. After a few minutes sitting with eyes closed, a trickle of tears began to flow.

"It's too hard. There are too many new things demanding my adjustment. It's an onslaught of stressors, like a spray of enemy bullets."

After I cried for ten minutes, the tears subsided. My eyes opened slightly. Two deep-seated eyes stared at me. They were just inches from my face. Terror fired through me as I saw large fleshy lips on a hairy body. A monkey sat facing me in a mirror image pose. All I could think of was rabies. A friend of mine had a daughter who died of rabies in India. "If I move, will it jump on me?" I wondered. I stood up slowly, drawing back a few feet in panic. The monkey grabbed the plastic bag with all my clothes and toothbrush in it. I swung to take it back. In a gesture of threat, the monkey showed huge fangs. "Will it attack? I don't know monkeys," I thought.

Echoes from the travel clinic about rampant rabies in India sent my adrenalin surging, showering stress hormones throughout my body. It was the antithesis of meditation.

When the monkey was distracted, I grabbed the bag and ran down the eight flights of stairs, tears streaming. I quickly sat at the foot of the stairs to join hundreds of composed, meditating, Buddha-like Hindus. We sat. Their white clothes were miraculously clean. Awareness that I was sitting on the ground by the bathroom door jolted me. I panicked again about germs. More echoes from the travel clinic: dengue fever, typhoid, hepatitis are epidemics in India. As I continued to sit in meditation, feeling extreme back pain, I remembered Swamiji's instruction:

"During meditation use *sukhasana*, cross-legged pose. No excuses. Back pain, no excuse. Knee operation, no excuse. If attention is on sense organs, meditation is not good. Little by little, forgive pain in body. Soon sit in full lotus position, *padmasana*. No exceptions. Otherwise, you are not meditating: just waiting until next birth to progress. Meditate at sunrise only. No excuse."

The tears continued streaming. Swamiji's assistant in orange robes came over to me.

"You're supposed to go there now," he said.

I opened my eyes. All the others had left. They were standing by an outside fire ceremony. I got up and joined the group.

I did not sponsor any *yagyas* in Mekedatu. I was afraid to ask for enlightenment again. I feared that this experience was the price I must pay for it. Some say meditation modifies *karma*, making it softer to bear.

I wondered if the *yagyas* I sponsored for rapid enlightenment were causing all my *karma* to be thrown at me at once, like a tornado.

To my chagrin, I remembered that back at the ashram I had sponsored a *yagya* to nullify seven lifetimes of *karma*. A fellow angel, a red-headed English woman named Rebecca, had been more skeptical. She compared the ashram to a spiritual Disneyland and the various *yagyas* to different rides. The greater the price tag for sponsoring a particular *yagya*, she reasoned, the more colorful and exciting the resulting experience for the sponsor. However, she had not "bought tickets." She was also having a much easier time in Mekedatu.

Swamiji's voice came to mind: "Do not compare yourself with other devotees. Do not look at other devotees. Each experience is different. Do not compare Swamiji with other gurus. Swamiji has so many forms."

I was still smarting from the hurt when Swamiji seemed to push me away. I felt his concerned gaze at one point in Mekedatu, but I refused to look at him.

"I will not be hurt like that again," I thought. Still, I could feel the softness of his aura.

Breakfast. I could not eat. Some *chai*—tea with milk and spices. "The heat will kill the germs on the glass," I thought. It was soothing but too sweet. I was sure that a clear message had come from the stars the night before not to eat sugar. I relented, desperate for comfort.

CHAPTER 9

In Over My Head

It is one thing to look at the country of peace from a mountaintop above the forest and another to hold to the path that leads there.

— Saint Augustine

"Mental states in which Swamiji lives and you live are very different. Swamiji travels in many different worlds and countries. Should not take personal if Swamiji looks at you or does not look at you. Swamiji very busy in many worlds. You must always try to be with Swamiji. Your attention on Swamiji is important, not Swamiji's attention on you. Don't sorrow. Don't upset. Swamiji has many duties, many worlds."

As I listened to Swamiji speak these words in class, I wondered if he was talking directly to me. Was he putting the perceived slight that I magnified so enormously into perspective? No matter. I was sick of the sternness.

There was not a chair in the entire prayer hall. I sat in my assigned spot on the floor, wedged in with the hundreds of other cross-legged sitters. The pain from a herniated disc I had had was becoming excruciating. I was angry. My brain was not working. I had lost the ability to retain new information. The memory machine was broken; the imprinting mechanism was out of commission, like the electricity that went off periodically in Mekedatu—the precious electricity that created hot, germ-free water.

I lost all sense of reverence. Who was this person talking endlessly in a language I could not understand? Occasionally he threw out rare sentences in English.

"They are tokens for the angels," I thought. "Crumbs for the dogs. I am angry at Swamiji. He is torturing me with pain."

The microbes had taken over: it was pointless for me to try to take in any new information.

I wondered, "Do I have encephalitis? Protein deprivation from days of nothing but rice?" At meals, I refused buttermilk, the only protein. "Avoid all dairy," they said at the travel clinic. "Nothing is pasteurized."

I had skipped many meals. There was no hunger. I ate only to try to stay warm, to endure the cold at night.

Swamiji's voice in class:

> Who complains is not fit for *kriya* yoga. Europeans come here. So many gurus. They have so many different gurus. So many illusions. Want sudden enlightenment from guru's touch. Short way to *moksha* [enlightenment] is not good. Long way is good. Guru is not responsible. *You* are responsible. Yoga has only one lesson: keep on practice. Sadguru helps. Don't disappoint. Don't depression. Real yoga: follow, follow, follow. Until death. Finish the game.

> All Europeans have same problem—too sensitive. Not like Indian people. Americans even worse. So many dreams. So many illusions. Don't study all books. Limitation. Full, small mind. Different ideas. Different gurus. Limitation very important. Must be moderation in learning also. Innocence means keeping mind pure—untainted state. Should not be corrupted by external feeding too much or mind loses strength. Americans read so many books—like so many millions of ants. After only three days most Americans go home.

"I am being personally humiliated," I thought, feeling enraged and defeated. "I am the only American here. With the flick of a finger, he has annihilated the value of my life and my hard-earned Ph.D. And, yes, I do want to go home, but I don't know how to get out."

The pain was radiating down my legs and spine. The cough was going deeper.

"I am sick. I cannot defend myself," I thought. "I've taken vitamin C and herbs, and the mucous grows greener. Should I take the antibiotics? If I take them, will I be immune when I need them for something more menacing?"

At the airport in the States, at the last moment before boarding the plane for India, I got medical evacuation insurance. It came with contact phone numbers of recommended doctors and hospitals in each city in India. No hospitals or contact doctors were even listed in Mysore where the ashram is located.

"But in Mekedatu? Where are we? We are nowhere. There is no time. There is no space. There is no town. It is wilderness. I could die here. Swamiji might think death-threatening sickness is good."

I remembered his voice from class:

> If problem is coming tomorrow say, "No. Come today my problems." Bring problems now. If problems coming later that day, say, "No. Don't come later. Come now, problems." Finish *karma* now. Finish the game. So many lifetimes. Birth. Death. Rebirth. Death. Rebirth. Death. So many births. This lifetime just preparation for next lifetime. Enough. Must have proper attitude toward problems. Some are *karma*. Don't sorrow my problems. Follow the master. Faith in God. Face the devil. Finish the game. Please finish the game. Say, "I'm fed up with always taking the human form."

My precious last bastion of safety—little foil-packed antiseptic wipes—were running out. I wiped cups and hands before eating, as per travel clinic recommendations. Hand washing with contaminated water was no help. Sparingly, in a miserly way, I used them for toilet paper.

One of the priests instructed us to place a red dot or sandalwood paste over the third eye. This was to keep the energies developed through yoga and meditation from dissipating. "This is very important," he urged. "And always meditate on a straw mat rather than directly on the floor or ground. Otherwise, spiritual energies from meditation flow out into the earth and are lost."

A group of men in the temple laughed at me when I took red *kum kum* powder with my left hand to apply to my third eye. They grabbed my hand before I could apply it, insisting I use my right hand. The left hand is for more unsanitary purposes. I could not get rid of the image of filthy left hands contaminating the right hands that prepared my food.

I dared to eat lunch. A woman told me about the nutritious value of the sprouted lentils in the meal. To make her point better, she grabbed a handful from my plate. She rubbed the food between her thumb and forefinger and dropped it back on my plate. My capacity to eat was destroyed. I delivered my plate to a squatting barefoot woman. She cleaned the plate with a hose and piled it with others on the dusty ground.

CHAPTER 10

Why Can't I Trust?

There is nothing that wastes the body like worry, and one who has any faith in God should be ashamed to worry about anything.
— Mahatma Gandhi

I was dreading the impending aching from cross-legged sitting as I went to the prayer hall for the afternoon session. During class rain started pouring with might—our blankets were on the roof. The angels bolted from the hall and charged up to the rooftop to salvage them. Although retrieved quickly, they were damp and cold. Two monkeys jumped onto the rooftop and headed for someone's bag. They snarled and showed threatening fangs when an angel tried to take it away. Still grimacing with fangs bared, a monkey slipped its hand deftly into the bag. It instantaneously pulled out a package of crackers. There was no searching, no digging in the bag. It was a monkey with psychic yogic powers, trained on Swamiji's roof. I did not have the cognitive categories for filing this experience. Monkey theft? Monkey yogi? Monkey *karma*? Monkey criminal? Simply, a nasty, little creature?

Later, from the rooftop the sun was setting behind the river, coloring the sky in bands of crimson. A mother monkey nursed her baby on the roof of Swamiji's quarters. It was a symbol of nurturance—something soft amidst the ongoing assault on my being. From afar, the monkeys were intriguing. They had fingers and fingernails. Their faces changed expression. Up close, I was afraid. They were unpredictable. I remembered Swamiji's words from Baton Rouge:

"Don't upset. Don't afraid. Free."

The baby monkey appeared when I was alone on the rooftop the next morning. It pulled at the dirty shawl I was wearing.

"Don't afraid. Free," I thought.

I introduced myself.

"*Jai Guru Datta*, Monkey," I said, using the phrase that universally echoed throughout the ashram—Hail to Guru Datta. It was used to mean hello, thank you, thank God.

"I'm Michael. I'm afraid because I don't know monkeys, but I like you," I said.

When the monkey picked more at the shawl on my shoulders, however, I ran down the stairs.

The blankets were wet that night. The eight of us packed into our tiny sleeping spaces on the roof, elbows almost touching.

We stared into the diamond-studded sky.

"This is our four star hotel," said one of the angels.

"No," said the German girl. "It's a multi-star hotel. Tell us a bedtime story."

I made up a story of Ganesh, the elephant god.

"Ganesh is riding on two monkeys instead of his usual mouse. He comes up on the rooftop. He uses his trunk like a hair dryer. He blows warm air and dries all the blankets. Then he takes his trunk and blows away all the beetles. Ganesh hovers over all the sleeping angels like a down comforter and keeps them very warm."

In spite of wet blankets, I slept that night. It was the only night that cold did not force me awake many times to drink hot water with hope.

Next dawn all sat in meditation outside Swamiji's house. I felt him approaching, even with my eyes closed. I knew that aura of softness. Still, I was raw with pain.

"Please don't hurt me," I said in my mind.

He stood next to me.

"Eyes half open," he said. "Open eyes half open."

Stern, but he didn't hurt me. Then I felt a quick, short tap between my eyebrows. He had flicked his finger on my third eye.

Later that morning in class, I noticed a little bit of clarity. I even laughed once. "Is the siege subsiding? Maybe I will be able to remember something this morning," I thought.

"Why can't I simply trust? Isn't this a holy place? Am I not protected?"

The thick, green mucous defied this notion. And who would believe that sitting cross-legged could be such profound torture?

By afternoon the clarity dissolved. I was back in the thick, green pea soup, spun upside down in the mealy waves. My memory was gone. My comfort was gone. My anchors were gone. What day was it? How many days remained? I wanted to go home. I missed my cats.

Swamiji's voice:

"Always you think you are missing something. You think you are missing your family. You think you are missing your friends. You think you are missing coffee. You are missing only one thing: you are missing God. You must pray. You must cut out idea of guru friendship. You must not think of guru as human being."

CHAPTER 11

Filthy River/Scary Saint

You must go through your karma until it is finished.
— Sri Ganapati Sachchidananda Swamiji

The lunch line barely moved. I stood patiently and then discovered it was not a lunch line after all. The group was going to the canyon where Swamiji's mother gave birth.

"A van will take us," someone said.

We walked. The road was wide. Heavy boughs with different hues of green formed a canopy shading the dirt road. After walking twenty minutes, we came to a river. There was no van. The water was choppy and grey, and there was no boat either. Women hiked up their skirts and began walking through the river to the other side. I had only one pair of shoes. I reluctantly took them off. There was no choice but to take them off. On the other hand, the course organizers warned us of broken glass in the river. The gentleness of the soothing, warm water

60

lessened my fears. I came out onto the opposite bank, my white clothes covered with mud.

The travel clinic had warned, "The water is contaminated. The rivers are contaminated. There are parasites in the water. If you go in the Ganges or other rivers, immediately dry off and rub alcohol all over yourself." However, my special rubber shoes for the river were four hours away in the ashram. I had no towel for brisk drying off, no alcohol for incipient parasites.

We walked another twenty minutes and came to a canyon through which a river ran. This was the birthplace, and it was beautiful. Swamiji's mother had been standing near a rocky cave in this river. A wave washed over her, and Swamiji was born.

A van arrived stuffed to the gills. Indian people offered their seats, even offered to pay the fare for angels. They are a very giving people. How sad that I could not simply relax and enjoy.

The bus took us to another part of the river where Swamiji was to join us. The special blessed event for the day was bathing in the river with Swamiji. I waited in the sun, covered with mud. I yearned for a shower. Images of burrowing parasites snaked through my mind. Finally, Swamiji arrived. I imagined I had already done my bathing and would stay on the river bank. I had not. Someone handed me turmeric and told me to smear it on my face.

Swamiji waded far out into the river, dressed in his sherbet orange robes. Water to the level of the knees was not sufficient. The procedure was to submerge completely. The group queued up and approached Swamiji. He was now far from shore. When I approached him, he filled a bucket with river water and poured it on my head. This is supposed to be a great blessing. I could only think of quickly getting into the shower. Pushing against the water with my legs I walked back to the shore, the press of the water resisting my desire for speed. The muddy river bottom squished up between my toes.

I left early and walked for about twenty minutes back to the showers. I was grateful for shampoo, for soap, for cold water. My feet were hurting. I investigated and discovered a small, bleeding cut. People began banging on the shower door. I tried to get the muddy stains out of my white pants to no avail. The banging continued. "I know there are many people, but I am so filthy," I thought. Black, gritty soot filled the cuffs created when I rolled up my pants to cross the river. "My white pants are filthy." My shoe polish-stained shawl only bled more in response to my soapy ministrations to it. "The Indian women always look so clean and beautiful. I am a wreck," I thought.

In the prayer hall that evening, my back and leg pains intensified as I sat. I tried not to extend my legs because I had heard it is an insult if done in the direction of the guru. "But is he even my guru? It doesn't matter. He is a holy man, that I know. He is a strict, demanding holy man who does not like me, who is intolerant of the need for comforts infused into my cells by a life of physical indulgences," I thought.

My foot began to hurt terribly. Having been broken twice, it always caused problems when I walked on uneven ground. I had walked a couple of hours on uneven ground and through an uneven riverbed. An area the size of a fist hurt where I cut my foot. It was too big an area for so small a cut. It hurt even when I put no pressure on it. "Has an infection taken hold?" I wondered. After dinner, I searched for the splinter of offending glass. Was this hunt exposing my foot to even more unfamiliar, lethal germs? How could I simply discount the need to be cautious, even phobic, about germs when sickness and thick, green mucous coursed through my body?

CHAPTER 12

The Empty Path to God:
Collapsing into Fullness

Your joy is your sorrow unmasked.

— Kahlil Gibran

With each day, I became weaker. I was increasingly out of breath as I climbed the eight flights to the rooftop. The roots of the cough grabbed hold deeper.

"Will this bronchitis become pneumonia? Is it already pneumonia? Will I die in India?" I wondered.

The electric power went off. With it, I lost my link to hot water for my thermos—my germ-free security and salvation from freezing cold when I repeatedly awoke in the night. My only socks were wet from washing after I waded in the river. I now walked barefoot. Each step was excruciating. The soles of my feet lacked the thickened skin of those accustomed to going barefoot. Still, it seemed impossible that it could be so painful simply to walk. "Has the very fiber of my feet been transformed into broken shards of glass?"

At the evening meeting Swamiji said:

"Swamiji gives blessing, but Swamiji is very busy. Don't upset like that. You must be happy. The ego must kill. So that is Swamiji's job. The ego must kill like a coconut. Like a strong coconut, we are cutting out. You benefit when Swamiji scolds you. He makes effort in order to bless you. You say, 'Thanks for scolding.' Then he has compassion on you."

I sat in my cross-legged torture pose, having taken ibuprofen in preparation. Even for the worst headaches in the States, I rarely took anything. Here in Mekedatu, I took it in advance to endure the sitting. Still, I was in pain. My head was swimming, my clarity gone again. Music boomed through a deafening tower of loudspeakers.

On this last evening in Mekedatu, the expansive music Swamiji played swept me into the vastness of space where I drifted among the stars. I floated through galaxies surrounded by gently spinning planets—Saturn with its rings, blue Venus.

Then, in the midst of the planets, in the center, at the point of stillness in the inky darkness of space, I saw Swamiji. He stood unmoving and totally composed. He held his right hand upright before his chest in a gesture indistinguishable from that of the teaching Christ. Through his absolute silence and by mere intention, Swamiji was orchestrating the integrated harmony of the cosmos. He maintained the perfect turning of celestial spheres on their axes and exquisitely balanced the forces of repulsion and attraction, keeping each planet in its rightful place. The unhurried planetary motions reflected the perfectly orderly resonance of his being, his absolute oneness powering their steady spinning, guiding them along unwavering orbits. I saw the divinity of natural law. I understood better that to be in tune with natural law is to be one with God's will.

The music built to a feverish pitch. It was very loud. Under Swamiji's baton, all two hundred people began to chant *OM*. Intensifying music, growing to a deafening volume, like the THX sound demonstrations in

U.S. movie theaters, accompanied the chanting. There was no end to the crescendo. My mind, my ears reached their limit of endurance. The sound went on building louder. Still it escalated. It was more than I could bear. Tears cascaded down my face. It was a flood of tears. My being was collapsing, crumbling in on itself.

The pain in my legs was excruciating. "I will myself to bear it." I thought. I had no more reserves with which to resist the suffering. "I am broken. The end is near. Each part of my body, every part of my being is broken."

My back bent forward. I collapsed in a pile, my face touching the wet floor. I was sobbing. "I will not move my legs away from the pain." Even resistance had left. It had not served me anyway. I could only accept the agony.

"There is nothing left to break. There is no *me* left to walk out of this room." I endured the torture without moving. I felt my being expand through and beyond the excruciating pain. "I am Christ on the cross. I am Christ's last breath."

Inexplicably, my Christian roots were coming to the fore. "I am one with the Father. I am no more. There is only God. I surrender. I surrender to God."

When finally I lifted my head, the hall was empty. People had long before filed past the heap on the floor.

CHAPTER 13

Guru Grants Highest Initiation

> *Endurance is one of the most difficult disciplines,*
> *but it is to the one who endures that final victory comes.*
> — Buddha

The next morning was the last day of the course. The Indians were abuzz about the events of the night before, when the deafening OM summoned my personal surrender.

"Last night, when Swamiji told the class to repeat the Sanskrit words *Tat Tvam Asi,* he gave us the highest initiation a living guru can grant."

Tat Tvam Asi, means "That alone you are. You are that only"—the teaching that you and God are one. There is no difference. You are *not* two. That alone is non-dual bliss. Thou art Brahman: you are one. That alone is liberation.

I was stunned. The price I had paid for this gem, however, still left me raw. The destruction of my small self, ego, accomplished my merging. While I sat in the prayer hall that final morning Swamiji's assistant approached me. I had seen him demonstrate pretzel-like yoga poses and breathing techniques for the class. He was a doctor.

"Swamiji told me to give you medicine for your cough." This tender gesture from Swamiji touched me. Swamiji, who seemed so stern and unfeeling, was, aware of and concerned about my illness after all. Out of a group of two hundred, he knew that I was sick. I took the medicine with gratitude. I was surprised that it was not an Ayurvedic (Indian medicine) herb, but a Western antibiotic. Within a few days, the illness subsided.

Later that day, during our final meeting in Mekedatu, Swamiji called us up before him, one by one. He held a crystal on a thick silver chain in his hands. As each person stood before him, he unhurriedly rotated the oval crystal as if programming it with some individualized protection or teaching. Then he presented each person with the silver necklace containing a similar crystal.

Usually Swamiji only allows devotees to touch his empty sandals placed at a distance from him. I heard that when devotees touch his feet, he takes on their stress and *karma*. After handing out each necklace, Swamiji permitted the course participant to bow and do just this— touch his feet. It felt like a graduation ceremony, Indian style.

When we finished, Swamiji said,

"Please remember in your dreams. Do not forget this place. We are all guru brothers and sisters. So many people wanted to come on this course, but Swamiji picked only you. Some people think accident they are here. No accident. Swamiji picked. Have strong faith. That is very important. Devotion. Follow. Love. Affection. Faith. Strong faith. Swamiji will help you in your meditation. Swamiji will help you in your *sadhana* (spiritual practice). Don't forget *kriya* yoga classes. Don't forget Swamiji. Don't forget yourself. People say Mekedatu is Swamiji's birthplace. It is not guru's birth place. It is *your* birthplace. Today you were born in Mekedatu."

CHAPTER 14

Back Home at the Ashram

At the root of all desire and fear is the feeling of not being what you are. Just as a dislocated joint hurts only as long as it is out of place, and is forgotten as soon as it is set right, so is all self-concern a symptom of mental distortion which disappears as soon as one is in the normal state.
— Sri Nisargadatta Maharaj

With profound gratitude that I was leaving Mekedatu, I boarded the bus to the ashram.

Swamiji is the reincarnation of Lord Dattatreya, the incarnation of Brahma, Vishnu, and Shiva. I found out later that Lord Dattatreya gave his disciples severe tests, almost beyond the limits of human endurance. In killing the coconut of my ego, Swamiji had almost killed me. Yet, in the end, as I dissolved in my pain into nothingness, feeling my destruction complete, I became aware of God's fullness. Even in this Hindu setting, my Christian roots, which I thought I had left behind, flew to the forefront of my awareness. On an experiential level, Christ merged with my pain, and through him, I experienced God. From a Hindu point of view, one could say, when the ego or belief in a self separate from God collapses, God fills all the spaces which the illusory self had usurped.

In the West, the word "ego" is linked to "egotism." As a result, Westerners may erroneously believe the Hindu goal of getting beyond the ego is a moralistic injunction to stop being selfish. It is not. Death of the ego in the Hindu paradigm is not an act of will or deliberate change of behavior. Rather, it is a cognitive shift, a realization that the individual self is an illusion. Just as a jar puts boundaries on the air it contains, breaking the glass removes the illusion of separateness: it contains the same air that is everywhere. To put excessive emphasis on the glass container rather than on the air, or to identify the human as separate rather than as a drop of the larger ocean of consciousness, is the essential error that transcending the ego negates. To focus on the individual body, personality or self places artificial boundaries on the universal soul or consciousness expressed in it.

The lesson of Hinduism is that the soul or consciousness has no separate identity despite temporary, dispensable boundaries created by the glass bottle or the human body. To "kill the ego" is to shatter the container to bring about awareness that we are one with God, with consciousness. Afterwards, one still functions as an individual but no longer harbors the illusion of separateness.

I am not sure how enduring this feeling of oneness with God achieved in Mekedatu was. Nor am I really sure how much the experience enhanced my spiritual evolution. The onslaught of stressors may even have set me back a few years. Indeed, according to the Transcendental Meditation paradigm, it is deep, peaceful rest of the nervous system allowing release of stored stress that maximizes growth toward enlightenment. In retrospect, it seems that, while the gradual release of stress as a daily backdrop enhances evolution, it may take extraordinary circumstances and experiences, like those in Mekedatu, to break the most entrenched, unyielding beliefs and habits that block evolution. As such, Mekedatu may have been the rare but necessary "surgery" required to remove the most unyielding block on my spiritual path.

What I clearly did gain in Mekedatu was profound appreciation and gratitude for simple comforts. I felt I could write a treatise to rival Descartes proving the existence of God based on the existence of chairs. I found myself waxing rhapsodic over the clean Western bathroom in Angel Hall. Had anyone yet written an ode to a toilet? I felt effusively appreciative of my dormitory bed at the ashram, both when in it and when admiring it from afar. Its mosquito netting was a luxury so precious it filled me with joy. And, oh, toilet paper from heaven! The warmth of four walls surrounding me and the pleasure of undisturbed sleep without cold awakening me multiple times in a night delighted me. The gratitude, which at first had a tinge of desperation to it, did not leave my side in the ensuing weeks. I gained access to it easily and often.

I composed variations on its theme, finding even more grounds to be thankful in different areas of my life. Indeed, the seeds of gratitude planted in India were sprouting up all over.

No doubt I had been through spiritual boot camp. As a result, I developed an enduring, more disciplined, and crisper approach to my *sadhana*. Instead of leaning in all directions using a back support, I assumed a straight-backed, cross-legged triangular posture during each meditation. Yoga *asana* postures, which I had left behind years before, became a daily prelude to my meditation. In the mornings, I began routinely snorting salt water to clear nasal passages, and then did *pranayama* breathing exercises to still the mind and purify the subtle body. I was a better soldier on the spiritual warrior's path because of my Mekedatu experience. I also found men even more attractive. Enchanted lightness or greater bliss, however, I did not feel.

A friend once minimized Impressionist art comparing it to Rembrandt and other heavyweights by saying Impressionist art was like candy. My preconceptions about the spiritual experiences I would have in India were like a blend of candy and Hallmark cards. The reality was much more serious and disturbing. It shook my complacency. Through the squealing of my senses it showed me how divorced my notion of rising above the senses was from my actual total enslavement to them. Minor deviations in ambient temperature, in my customary mode of sitting, in the thickness of padding separating my body from the floor, and in whether soap washed my dishes caused me practically to disintegrate.

Naturally, I avoid thinking about Mekedatu for fear of reactivating the horror I experienced there. In my avoidance, however, I neglect to savor the diamond at the core of the experience—the brief experience of Being totally one with the divine—in a *feeling* sense, accompanied by direct perception of loss of individuation. I saw that the very substance of my being, my awareness, my consciousness was not separate from the vast field of consciousness that is God and which informs all of reality. Further, I saw that Swamiji was a manifestation of that same energy.

—◁▷—

Some days later, when I was again in the comfort of Angel Hall, an attendant called me to the front of the prayer hall. Swamiji handed me an orange scarf and a flat square made of cardboard. Only when I returned to my mat did I dare to look at it. At first, the dark glossy picture did not come into focus. As I turned it from side to side, I recognized a hologram with a three-dimensional figure. As I looked more closely, I saw brilliant stars in the darkness. In their midst stood Swamiji, his right palm facing outward, his hand upright at his chest. It was the same image Swamiji's music in Mekedatu had induced in me before my surrender. The holographic image of my meditation vision and the echoing remembrance of Swamiji's music fulfilled my love of the aesthetic. With gratitude, I clutched the picture to my heart. This objectification of my meditation vision of Swamiji in the spheres as a tangible hologram created a profound feeling and perception of wholeness. This personalized confluence of realities broke all boundaries of causality. In its transcending of the laws of time and space, the reduplicative experience embraced and expressed the power of the divine.

Some years later, I read Krishnamurthy's (1993) account of Swamiji's transformative experience at age twenty-four. It brought Swamiji to the "main phase" of his life. A few weeks before this transformation he had moved to the newly acquired ashram grounds. He slept outdoors under a mango tree because no buildings were constructed yet. Two devotees accompanied him on a journey to Srilalam Peak, a sacred spot and abode of Lord Dattatreya. Its very sight confers liberation of the soul. Swamiji plunged into the River Krishna and stayed under the water for a long time (to the consternation of the two devotees accompanying him.) There, Swamiji's externally directed mental behavior dissolved completely in the river, which washed it away. Ganesh, the elephant god, manifested in order to bestow knowledge to Swamiji, who was still under water. He told Ganesh of feeling uneasy because "things are progressing without my will." Ganesh replied that this was a happy thing. Swamiji said he feared there would be tests and an examiner. Then he recognized that the very idea that there is an examiner always causes fear. "The name of my ailment is fear." Ganesh asked him why fear arises. "On account of separateness. I have understood. I've understood my mistake," Swamiji said. With recognition that there is no separateness, Swamiji realized his oneness with the infinite.

When he came out of the water, filled with divine bliss, Swamiji told his devotees,

> This is the main phase in Swamiji's life history. In this body, a distinguished consciousness exists—a consciousness endowed with divine grace *par excellence*. That divine consciousness combines atoms with one another and also separates them. It is that divine consciousness that guides the moveable and immoveable worlds through rotations of the wheel of Time, upkeeping the path of eternal virtue. Its name is Swamiji—It is Swamiji to you, and to me as well.

This was the Swamiji among the stars captured in my meditation vision in Mekedatu and again in the hologram given to me of Swamiji, guiding worlds through their rotations.

One devotee asked him, "If everything is done by that Swamiji, what will you be doing?"

Swamiji answered:

No language in the world is adequate to reply to that query—to tell you within the means of expression that I will be observing each and every thing that goes on in this universe. So, some people call me a witness. . . Are you not calling the one in this body Swamiji? Hereafter I will also call him Swamiji.

Dating from this experience at age twenty-four Swamiji has always referred to himself in the third person.

Swamiji's transformational recognition that he was not separate from the Infinite included recognizing that he is one with the Force that guides the rotations of the worlds. Since my vision of him preceded my transformational recognition that the Father and I are one, I wonder if spiritual guides create variants of their own experiences in their disciples as a way of teaching.

CHAPTER 15

Reincarnated Tibetan Lama

T *he similarities are greater than the differences
between Hinduism and its derivative, Buddhism.
God is too big to fit inside one religion.*

The rest of my stay in India was gentle by comparison. One highlight was an excursion from the ashram to a Tibetan community, about an hour-and-a-half drive from the ashram. A Danish woman accompanied me. Jetta had been practicing Transcendental Meditation for more than twenty years. Just minutes before meeting Swamiji for the first time, she found herself sobbing. She had no idea why she was crying. Once she met him, however, she knew they were tears of gratitude and relief at finally having met him.

I strongly sensed that Swamiji was orchestrating our trip to the Tibetan settlement to provide some uniquely relevant experience. Years later, a renowned Indian astrologer Shastraji gave me a reading drawn from the Book of Bhrigu. The ancient seers, such as Bhrigu, amused themselves by drawing up the astrological charts of those not yet born who were destined to seek a reading from the Book of Bhrigu, a set of palm leaves inscribed with this information. Shastraji told me that in a previous lifetime I had lived in Tibet. My guru there had ousted me when I began exploring other religious groups, and I fled to Southern India. A family that was involved with Swamiji took me in. Thus, during my Tibetan lifetime I came to know Swamiji.

Some say that during our lifetime we gather parts of our soul from different places where we lived in previous lifetimes. I sensed that Swamiji organized my trip to the Tibetan community during my ashram stay, perhaps so that I could gather soul parts. My Tibetan connection with Swamiji may also have accounted for my spontaneously placing my forehead on Swamiji's sandals during my first meeting with him in Baton Rouge, a gesture I later learned was a Tibetan means of simultaneously expressing reverence and of getting blessings from the object revered.

Jetta and I negotiated a price with a cab driver who spoke some English. Then we set off for the Tibetan community of Bylakuppe. We traversed many bumpy, dusty miles of road through low, rolling green hills to the west of Mysore. We knew we were close when the faces in the streets began to change: they were rounder and softer, and the eyes more almond-shaped. After the Chinese invasion of Tibet, with its attendant massacres, many Tibetans fled to India. With the protection of the Indian government, they were allowed to set up refugee settlements where they guard many of their traditions. These settlements are reminiscent of American Indian reservations: bastions of a different culture and language, and with shops selling native handicrafts.

We stopped to ask a Tibetan man if there was a monastery in the community. Through some composite of Hindi, English, Tibetan, and Danish, we got directions.

The monastery was quite small. Two eager children with shaved heads and tiny ponytails got a key and took us to the temple. A dark-haired child unlocked the door of the building that looked like a small country church from the outside. Inside, the feeling was completely different. The silence and stillness were profound. Ancient *tankhas* (rectangular Tibetan images painted on cloth and framed by a narrow cloth border) adorned the walls. Centuries of chanting and sacred devotion suffused them and filled me with the feeling of reverence they exuded. I felt humbled by the presence of divinity. It was a privilege to be allowed in this private, sacred space used by the Tibetan monks living in this enclave. Before each *tankha* hung a candle, flickering steadfastly. An enormous painting of Buddha, more than eight feet tall, filled the center of the altar. We luxuriated in the enveloping silence.

A Tibetan monk appeared. He greeted us in limited English. The *thankas* and painting of Buddha had been smuggled out of Tibet before the Chinese could destroy them, he explained. The monk showed us to his small room to see a *thanka* he was painting. To the side I noticed a photograph of a small boy in maroon and gold robes.

"Is he the reincarnation of a *lama*?"

"Yes, he is," the monk said.

"Is it possible for us to meet him?" I said.

"He is not here. He lives in other monastery, in Sera."

"How far is that monastery?"

"About one hour from here," he said.

As we were leaving the grounds, a giant prayer wheel in a small hut caught our attention. It was about twenty feet high. It had spokes extending out about waist-high to the man in the hut. His job was to grab the spokes and spin the wheel. As he did so, he repeatedly chanted *Om mani padme hum*. This Tibetan mantra purifies and transforms negative emotions. Tibetan prayer wheels contain cylinders of rolled paper inscribed with hundreds of prayers. The spinning of the wheel activates the prayers within. When the man noticed my interest, he invited me to come in and take over spinning the wheel. After some joyful whirling, we boarded the waiting taxi and set off on a hunt to find the reincarnated *lama*.

We came to a nearby village, spotted a Tibetan monk, and asked him for directions to the monastery at Sera. When verbal directions would not suffice, given the multiple language barriers among us, the monk jumped in the cab and showed us the way. With his generous help, we arrived at the monastery, a sea of golden and maroon robes. Jetta and I were almost the only women among the thousands of robed monks.

One of the largest monasteries in Lhasa, Tibet, it was transplanted to India after the Chinese invasion. It is really a small town, with several streets and buildings, home to about 3000 monks in training at the monastic university on the grounds. They speed up and down the several streets, dividing their time between academic study and the practice of Buddhism. A kind monk understood after our gesticulations that we were looking for the reincarnated child *lama*. He led us down winding streets and delivered us to the attractive house with sumptuous gardens where the child lived.

We knocked on the door. A tall, fair-skinned monk in traditional robes greeted us in perfect English. He was an Australian who, drawn to Buddhism, had taken vows and was living at Sera.

"Hello," I said. "We're here visiting the monastery. We understand that the child *lama* lives here and wondered if it would be possible to meet him."

"Yes, he does live here. He's having his English lesson now. Let me see if he can meet with you later."

He disappeared leaving the door ajar. He returned in a few minutes.

"He'd be happy to meet with you," he said. "Can you return about four o'clock?"

"That would be fine."

Pleased with our progress, Jetta and I meandered around the grounds. We heard deep, reverberating sounds of two-tone chanting, Tibetan horns and the clinking-glass sound of Tibetan cymbals. We followed the sounds to their source, a room where about thirty monks were performing a *puja*. A monk motioned to us to come in and sit down. We sat on the floor, and listened to the rich, low-pitched sound of throat chanting. Each monk chanted two different tones simultaneously, making a deep, almost growling sound. The palpable vibration induced a state of meditation, transporting us to an ancient world where we floated for about an hour. Candles flickered in the dark room. The monks glided brass ritual objects through the air in sinewy patterns as they conducted a ceremony. At the end, they passed around a mysterious food—a dumpling of some sort, which we consumed. With *chakras* spinning, we left and made our way down the cobblestone streets to meet the baby *lama*.

Osel, no longer the child in the photo we had seen, was now thirteen years old. He was calm, socially poised, and curious to know about us. He asked with genuine interest where we were from and what brought us to India. Otherwise, he was ostensibly unremarkable. He told us about his pet deer. It was blind and lived in the garden. We shook his hand when we left. I was struck by the extreme softness of his touch. Perhaps it bespoke lifetimes of meditation.

As we were leaving the room, the Australian monk invited us to join him for tea on the veranda. Sitting surrounded by flowers and foliage, we talked about Buddhism for about an hour. We learned that at any one time there are about fifty reincarnated *lamas* on earth. "*Lamas*," the monk explained, "are just teachers. They are enlightened gurus."

He spoke of the hardships of many Tibetan monks who had barely escaped Tibet with their lives. Several had crossed the snowy Himalayas by foot in order to reach India. Once in India many had contracted tuberculosis and died.

He spoke of the compassion of the Tibetans for their oppressors, the Chinese. "This compassion is possible because we understand the role of *karma*. We understand the terrible *karma* the Chinese are incurring through their behavior."

He also spoke of the Buddhist signature concept of emptiness: "Everything is impermanent and changing—except the mind's constant labeling."

Drinking tea at this center of Tibetan thought and training in India tasted of eternity and magic. Our focus was enlightenment and Eastern philosophy. This education came not from printed words but through the vibrancy of maroon and saffron robes, a reincarnated child *lama*, and an eloquent spokesman for Tibetan Buddhism.

As our visit ended, the Australian monk and Osel's Tibetan attendant handed us a book. It told the story of Lama Yeshe and his reincarnation as Osel. Lama Yeshe was a Tibetan monk who had died about fifteen years before. The traditional series of tests established Osel's reincarnated authenticity. For example, as an infant he correctly identified, from an array of choices, the prayer bell, the rosary, and other objects that were his in the previous lifetime. The fair-skinned Osel was born in Spain and there identified. The Dalai Lama, the spiritual and political leader of the Tibetan people, verified that, indeed, he was the reincarnation of Lama Yeshe.

Lama Yeshe was known for his work in bringing Tibetan Buddhism to the West. He learned English and had many foreign disciples. His teaching methods were unconventional. For instance, to understand the culture of his Western students better, he donned loud beach attire and, on occasion, attended nightclubs. His nature was inquisitive. Genuine interest in and concern for people were hallmarks of his personality, traits I noticed in Osel.

We were so buoyantly satisfied by our spiritual adventure that we did not even react to the (objectively) harrowing taxi ride home. The lack of traffic lanes with the weaving back and forth of cars into oncoming traffic, animals, and people requires some adjustment during daylight hours in India. However, the nighttime driving we were subjected to is an altogether different experience. We drove for two hours on a violently pitted road filled with as many animals as people. The combination of no traffic lanes and no streetlights means that it is commonplace that oncoming headlights will blind you. These fleeting blinding episodes terminate in a sudden swerve negotiated at the last second. How this occurs is mysterious. The oncoming headlights presumably blind the driver while he is negotiating the swerve. No doubt, without the bliss from our spiritual *hegira* filling us, the experience would have been difficult. But the wild ride and yielding to the experience were a metaphor for the accelerating personal crisis in my enlightenment quest, which, I had learned, only surrender resolved.

A few years later, the Dalai Lama met with Swamiji at the ashram in Mysore. At that meeting, Swamiji released a newly published book of accounts of devotees' experiences with him. The book included a few pages which I contributed about the shifting of time and causality in Swamiji's presence. I have a cherished photograph of the Dalai Lama holding the book as Swamiji sits at his side. In retrospect, my visit to the Tibetan community was a Tibetan seed. The blessing of the Dalai Lama and Swamiji focusing on the book to which I had contributed was its fruition. In fact, it may have had its roots far earlier in my Tibetan lifetime.

One evening a few days later a German lady, Anasuya, rushed into the dormitory where I was just settling down with a good book.

"Hurry," she said. "Someone from the monastery where the Shankaracharya lives is next door. He is giving *darshan* for just a few minutes to a small group of people."

Anasuya was a teacher of Transcendental Meditation. Anyone practicing TM for any length of time soon learns of the importance of the Shankaracharya tradition which began with Adi Shankar. The role of this lineage of pontiffs, dating back to the sixth century B.C., is to embody and to safeguard the purity of Hindu teachings. The Shankaracharya of Jyotir Math in the North was the guru of Maharishi Mahesh Yogi. He instructed Maharishi to teach a form of meditation suitable for householders—the practice now known as Transcendental Meditation.

The first Shankaracharya, Adi Shankar, dedicated his life to safe-guarding Hinduism and to propagating the Advaita philosophy of non-dualism. He established four monastic institutions in India (called *maths*), each with its own Shankaracharya. He wrote commentaries on sacred texts, and nominated one of his disciples as the first *acharya* in each monastic institution, giving him instructions for founding a line of successive *acharyas* to continue this protective role.

Anasuya knew that I would cherish the opportunity to meet anyone somehow connected to the Shankaracharya. I followed her across the street and into a two-storey building. A tall, elderly Indian man was lying on his side on a divan, I presumed because of tiredness or delicate health. The ancient holy man had walked throughout much of India. Two people were kneeling in front of him. The fifteen people in the room spoke in hushed tones. Two assistants gestured to those entering to stand in line. When I approached the holy man, he handed me a pamphlet about the Kanchi Math, today one of the most influential, though it is not one of the original four *maths*.

A translator, speaking in a very loud voice directly into his ear, told him that I was from the United States. His face became very animated, and he dug his hand deep into a pile of tiny sugar cubes. He handed me a fistful of them as *prasad* which I later distributed to the Transcendental Meditation community where I live in Texas. Because of the huge handful of *prasad* he gave me, I sensed that he knew of my connection with the TM community.

Chapter 16

Tabla Playing

*The Lord respects me when I work,
but he loves me when I sing.*

— Shaker Saying

Back at the ashram we saw much less of Swamiji. At Mekedatu we had spent most of the day with him, but here we saw him regularly only at morning prayers. Sometimes after evening *bhajans,* Swamiji would step out on a balcony for two or three minutes to provide us a glimpse of him. The five days following our Tibetan outing were an exception. These were days of celebration, and Swamiji performed, playing music for hours every night.

"Music is my religion," Swamiji has said. Even from recordings, his music has healed people's ailments. Many devotees have come to Swamiji through first hearing his music. Only later did they discover the immense spiritual being who created it.

I delighted in sitting as close as possible and watching the amazing hand movements of the tabla player. His fingers moved faster than the eye could process. That morning I had read in a book by one of Swamiji's devotees a description of the freedom of schedule at the ashram. Apart from morning and evening prayers and *bhajans*, people spend the day as they please. Swamiji believes this freedom allows personal exploration of spirituality in the manner uniquely suited to each individual.

As I was sitting that evening listening to the music, I had a sudden flash to Swamiji's words, "You do some research in that," when I had asked him about pursuing music as a career. It occurred to me that there was no better way of doing research than experientially—by learning to play the *tabla*. The idea energized me, and I went to see Ramesh in the office. He agreed to arrange a meeting with Swamiji's *tabla* player so I could discuss lessons. I felt impatient because my remaining days at the ashram were dwindling.

When we finally met, he referred me to a music school that did not exist. I spoke to Ramesh again. Ever eager to please, he introduced me to another musician in Swamiji's entourage. He played the clay pot, an Indian instrument used like a drum. I had also seen him on stage playing with Swamiji each night during bhajans. His name was Manju. He had dark hair and large, dark eyes. His gaze was steady and his face kind but serious. I liked him immediately. After having seen his frenzied, rhythmic finger movements on the drums, I was surprised by the mellifluous quality of his voice.

"So you want to learn the *tabla,*" he said in a peppery Indian accent superimposed on the honey-sweet smoothness of his voice.

"Yes, I'd love to," I said.

"First, we have to get the blessings of Swamiji. Do you have an instrument?"

"No," I said.

"Will you ask Swamiji's secretary, Prasad, for Swamiji's permission tomorrow? I'll arrange for the instrument. We can meet tomorrow evening after *bhajans*." He looked at his watch and was gone.

I got permission, the purpose of which I didn't fully understand. In the afternoon, a knock on the door at Angel Hall announced the delivery of my *tabla*. The hammered silver drum and smaller wooden drum had skins laced to the tops with bright purple quilted pads tied to the laces for protection.

After *bhajans,* Manju and I walked over to Angel Hall. We found a small area with a grey slate floor. On the wall was a large poster of Swamiji, smiling and dressed in pink robes. A single transparent light bulb lit the dim room, which was bare but for an oddly shaped ironing board and an anachronistic-looking iron. For the remainder of my stay at the ashram, this was my music room.

Manju and I sat on the cool stone floor facing each other, the drums between us. He positioned my hands on the round leather skins, and our lessons began. At ten o'clock Manju stood up.

"I'll be back tomorrow morning at eight thirty to see how you're doing," he said.

"Isn't that going to be too much for you?" I said. I felt I was imposing on him and on the graciousness of India. "Don't you have to be at work?"

"I do have to be at work, but I'll stop here first to see your progress," he said.

I was appreciative of his taking his mentorship so seriously. It clearly implied the need for equal diligence on my part. For a while after he left I continued practicing. From my position on the floor, Swamiji seemed to be looking down at me with approval. The smile on his face contrasted with the sternness I had come to fear. After meditation and morning prayers, I hurried back to Angel Hall to practice before Manju arrived. At the end of our lesson he said,

"I'll be by tonight after *bhajans*, and we'll have another lesson."

So began our twice-daily *tabla* marathon.

"How did you meet Swamiji?" I asked once between drum beats.

"My father, who was also a musician, was a devotee of Swamiji. He played with Swamiji starting in 1973. He played music with him all those years until I took his place in 1991," he said.

"Well, it's a special honor having you teach me. I didn't realize that you and your father had been playing with Swamiji for so long."

Manju embodied all of the Indian qualities of generosity, steadiness, devoutness, and caring that I had come to admire. As a long-term devotee, he was a representative of Swamiji but without the sternness, the unpredictability, and the erratic attention toward me that I found so difficult. His devotion to Swamiji was very strong; he had been with him since he was a child. Through Manju, I could appreciate Swamiji vicariously. Manju came to feel to me like a good Indian father. The lessons provided for a successful meeting of East and West, a success I did not feel in Mekedatu. With Manju, my longstanding love of music allowed for carrying some familiarity into the newness. I brought my piano training, my good ear, and knowledge of rhythm that could then be dressed in the sounds of a new instrument.

"Tell me about Ganesh," I said early on, referring to the elephant-headed god known as the Remover of Obstacles.

"You must always pray to Ganesh before starting anything—before traveling, before working, before playing *tabla*. Before all these things, always pray to Ganesh."

Manju was patient and determined in his approach. After the morning lesson, he would ask my plans for the afternoon. If they included a foray into Mysore, he would say,

"Better you stay in and practice."

I had some clothes made and wanted to have them altered. Actually, I wanted to have them redesigned, which is quite within the realm of possibility in India. It was nearing the end of my stay, and I had a number of errands to do in Mysore. I was determined to go into town.

When Manju arrived that morning, he said, "The auto rickshaw drivers are on strike. It is a government strike. It has spread to some of the shops, too. Better you stay in and practice. Those who are on strike are angry with anyone who drives a taxi. If you take a regular taxi, you could be injured. You stay in and after strike is over, maybe tomorrow, maybe next day, then you can go shopping."

CHAPTER 17

Ayurvedic Medical Treatment
in India

*Health of body and mind is a great blessing,
if we can bear it.*
— John Henry Cardinal Newman

Several people at the ashram had heard about the American who was learning to play *tabla*. An Indian couple who had lived in Arizona asked me daily about my progress. In passing I mentioned that I loved to play, although sitting cross-legged was painful and that I had put turmeric paste on my knees to no avail. The husband, Selvam, was going to the Ayurvedic hospital at the ashram for treatments. The free clinic provided care and medicines for anyone in the city. He suggested I stop in and see the doctor. I resisted, feeling that only a dire emergency merited hospital attention. He finally persuaded me to go.

The clinic was a humble building with no frills. Two Indian doctors, one trained in Ayurveda and one in traditional Western medicine met with me. They took my pulse, had me fill out an extensive questionnaire, and then determined my body type. "Pain is usually caused by an excess of *vata* (air/movement) energy. Not enough *vata*, however, is causing your pain," the doctor said.

She recommended a week of daily oil massages, steam baths, and some herbs. "Here is a prescription for the medicated oils and for the herbs. Come tomorrow morning at 6:00 AM in your night dress and bring the oils. After your massage you can bathe here and dress to go to the prayer hall." As I walked out of the office I met an elderly Indian woman.

"My name is Meera," she said. "I'm an inpatient here at the hospital. Are you coming for treatment?"

"Yes, I'm coming tomorrow morning."

"Very good. I think you will have good results. My daughter took me to so many doctors for this back pain. Nothing was helping, and I said, 'I'm not going to any more doctors.' But then she convinced me to come here. Only this treatment has helped. I can stand up straight for the first time in two years."

Meera's remarks encouraged me. Maharishi had introduced me to Ayurveda, which recognizes different body types and their corresponding different diets and treatments to maximize health. I had had Ayurvedic treatments in the United States, but they were expensive, and I hadn't kept them up.

The next morning I set out from Angel Hall before the sun rose. I arrived at the hospital building and found the door bolted shut. I knocked. There was no response; I banged harder. After about ten minutes, a sleepy attendant answered the door. The emerging dawn light illuminated her face, but behind her the interior of the building was in total darkness. I tried to explain that I had come for a scheduled massage. She told me something in Telugu, but I didn't understand. Then Meera appeared and translated.

"The power has gone off," she said. "So there won't be any steam for the steam bath or hot water for your bath afterwards. You should come back tomorrow morning. You can leave your oils in my room if you like, so you don't have to bring them back and forth."

She showed me to her modest room. A piece of neatly folded newspaper served as a mat on the bedside table. On it was a bottle of water and a cup, the only familiar hospital room accouterments. There were no screens on the windows. A spiral of foul-smelling chalky substance was burning by the window to ward away mosquitoes.

India provides many opportunities for transcending judgment and for learning flexibility and patience. I returned the next morning, and although the power was back on, my knocking again served as the alarm clock to wake up the staff. The attendant, her hair not yet combed and her eyes sleepy, motioned me to wait in the hall. There were no chairs. I gestured to request one, and she returned with a chair a few minutes later. As I waited I could feel my patience dwindle. I began to meditate. When I finished I looked at the clock and realized I would miss the morning prayer meeting unless the massage started soon. I communicated this through Meera who was in the middle of having a massage herself. Time urgency carries no weight in India. Everyone at the clinic politely ignored mine.

After another twenty minutes, Meera got up from the large wooden table which had an elevated lip around the edges. It was covered with oil used during her massage. The attendants took the bottle of medicated oil I got from the pharmacy and motioned me onto the wet table. I reassured myself that bacteria probably could not live in oil. This was likely an inaccurate notion, but its inaccuracy served me well in fending off the growing sense of repulsion as I was sliding onto the slimy table. The attendants poured on some oil and began kneading me as though I were a sourdough loaf in the making. Privacy and modesty have a very different flavor in India, I learned. Various staff people wandered in and out and spoke to the masseuses as they worked on me.

After half an hour they escorted me to a large wooden box with a hole on top. It reminded me of the outdoor containers for bagged ice in front of many stores in the States. They opened the door and told me to sit with my head protruding from the hole. But my shoulders were jamming into the top of the box. This problem was corrected when they spun down the seat of the stool on which I sat. Next to the box was a hot plate with a pot of boiling water. A rubber hose from the lid of the pot into the box provided steam. I felt absurdly out of my element as I sat with my head prepared for the guillotine. My oily body slipped and slid on the wheeled stool that rolled whenever I inadvertently moved on the seat. The slow jet of steam threatened to boil the flesh of my leg, so I was careful to repeatedly readjust my position.

After my steam bath I was directed to walk through the men's ward in my half-clad state to where I was to have my bath. I passed rows of beds filled with inactive men whose major occupation was watching the activity in the aisle between the beds as people occasionally passed through.

The bath was in a dark, closet-sized room. It seemed to be a mop room. Hanging over a rack to dry was jumbo-sized enema equipment that looked like it could blow away intestines. There was a drain in the center of the uneven grey floor. A residue of oil and God knows what else plastered the dark grey walls and floor. With the door closed, it was almost pitch black because there was no electric light in the room. An attendant met me and filled a pail with hot water from something that looked like a large electric coffee urn. She handed me the filled pail along with a plastic cup. This combination was my shower, the mop room my shower stall. Had I not been in the ashram I might have simply fled. But because I was in India on a spiritual quest, I viewed my experiences as lessons and tests. The humble outward trappings were a call to see beyond to the kindness infusing the clinic and to the help given patients.

Initially, I found the mop room awkward and repugnant. I adapted over the course of the week, however, and became quite adept at soaping up and rinsing off with a pail of water. I appreciated the scalding water, hotter than any water at Angel Hall. However, I never got used to walking half-clad through the men's ward, where I once passed my fellow devotee, Selvam, receiving a therapeutic enema. I looked away, wishing we had not had the opportunity to share this bizarre moment of intimacy. He, however, seemed unperturbed as I and others filed by. Ironically, it was the last time I saw Selvam before I left India. This final view of an acquaintance is, without doubt, the strangest stored in my memory bank.

CHAPTER 18

Preparing to Leave, Pulled to Stay

*P*atience is the greatest penance.
— *Sri Ganapati Sachchidananda Swamiji*

My plans to travel around India began dissolving of their own accord. The thought of leaving the ashram early was losing its appeal. A few days before I was to go on a safari, Swamiji announced that he was going to take the angels to the zoo. He asked us to contribute to covering animals' food and zoo keepers' salaries for a day. The request brought to mind my cats: I reasoned that supporting the zoo animals would bring protection to my cats at home. The jaunt to the zoo satisfied my safari yearning, further quelled by the thought of being in a tent at the mercy of malaria-bearing mosquitoes.

Further, my forays to crowded local temples had become unsatisfying, completely extinguishing my desire to tour the rest of India. At one temple, for an extra fee, the curator dimly lit the otherwise imperceptible sculptures. He carried a light that stretched the length of

91

a short extension cord, so only those carvings within the range of the cord could be seen, leaving many invisible. He also shooed away the massive crowds of sightseers who had not paid the additional fee. The presence of these elbowing crowds detracted from any sense of sanctity within the temple.

Each day I continued to postpone my departure. I was not only running low on funds, which I kept spending on *pujas* and other ashram events, but I was still engaged in my *tabla* lessons and was motivated to finish my course of Ayurvedic treatments.

My experience with Ayurvedic herbs in the United States had always been either inconsequential or very subtle, so I did not expect to feel much effect from the herbs I got from the clinic. However, on first taking Ayurvedic herbs, I had a dramatic response. I was sitting in the prayer hall while Swamiji played music. Layer by layer, I could feel the pain dissolve, replaced by a sensation of light filling my cells. Unfortunately, the pain returned the next day, but I felt that the herbs and the music had initiated some positive healing process.

—✠—

The intricate spiraling patterns in Indian sculpture and fabric are an apt reflection of life in India, which is never simple, linear, or direct. For example, on my way out of India I wanted to see Karunamayi, the Indian saint I had seen in Houston. Her ashram is in Bangalore where I would catch my return flight to Bombay. I had the phone number and address of the ashram and wanted to call to get permission to visit.

Indian phone booths are about the same shape as those in the United States. They are pale blue in color, and made of metal rather than glass. I waited for about thirty minutes for the previous caller to finish. I entered the small booth and, to my astonishment, I discovered another person sitting in it. She was the operator, separated from me by a partial wall. She asked me to tell her the number, which she dialed. Then she handed me the receiver over the wall. I could not help but wonder how it could be too expensive to put toilet paper in each bathroom, but affordable to put an operator in each phone booth. Musing, I held the receiver and listened to the ringing. Hearing a voice, which sounded like a recording in an Indian dialect, I handed the receiver back to the operator. "All the circuits in Bangalore are busy," she said.

Over the next hour in the steamy cabinet, we finally got through to Bangalore. The cramped quarters, the waiting, and the insanity of being in such a tiny space with another person made me feel like screaming. I was sick and tired of trying to accept as normal all of the many things, which, from an entrenched perspective I was unwilling to yield, were clearly abnormal. As I was fuming, the operator informed me that the ashram phone was not working. I asked if we could call Information, known as "Inquiries" in India, to get the correct number. "Inquiries," however, was busy. After another thirty minutes of repeated calls, the operator suggested I come back the next day.

Similar fruitless telephone rituals consumed my time for several days. An Indian recommended I speak with a travel agency for assistance with contacting Karunamayi's ashram. When I called the agency, they insisted I come into the office, adding to my irritation. They sent a car to pick me up when I told them the striking auto rickshaws blocked my coming. The travel agency's FAX to the ashram yielded a response. There were no sleeping accommodations at the ashram, but they recommended a Bangalore hotel. The travel agency booked a room.

A few days later in preparation for my departure I went to cash traveler's checks at the bank. After waiting in line for nearly thirty minutes, a sleepy clerk told me to go and Xerox my passport.

"Can't you do it here?" I said, irritation mingling with astonishment.

"No," he said. "We don't have facilities for copying here."

"Where can I have it done?" I said, feeling contagious resignation wash over me.

"At the police station down past Chamundi Street."

After asking numerous passers-by, I found the police station. It was two flights up in a building under construction. An even sleepier clerk in uniform awaited, seated at a lone desk.

"Could you please make a copy of my passport for me?"

"Oh, no, Madam. I cannot," he said. "I am not *authorized.*"

I explained my plight to no avail. When it was clear that he would not yield and make a copy, I said,

"Where can I go to get a copy?"

"Only the Commissioner of Police can make a copy."

I felt like I was in a movie. I *was* in a movie, the movie that is India.

"You cannot walk," he said. "You would spend nearly the whole day walking. It is better you take auto rickshaw."

After a thirty-minute ride past yoked oxen and bent men carrying loads rivaling those pulled by the oxen, I arrived in a section of town with wide, relatively empty streets. We pulled up to a palatial estate. Two gun-wielding uniformed guards with decorative helmets stood on either side of an iron gate. They allowed me to pass without a word.

When I found my way to the Commissioner's office, he was as dumb-founded as I was that I had come to his quarters to have something Xeroxed. Although India abounds with computers used even in the ashram for scheduling *pujas,* Xerox machines are as rare as hen's teeth. I acknowledged full understanding to the Commissioner that Xeroxing was not part of his function in protecting the populace. In the interest of my getting a check cashed before the bank closed, however, I convinced him to arrange for the copying of my passport. He sent someone out with the passport. I continued standing, expecting to leave in a minute or two. As the minutes far exceeded two, I could feel my blood beginning to boil. A quote from Swamiji, painted on the wall of the ashram came to mind: "Patience is the greatest penance."

This sparked a further remembrance, which I wished had not visited me. The last time I'd gone for Swamiji's blessing I had nothing to put in the offering basket. When I realized this, too late, I thought, "I'll offer my impatience when standing in line. That should be more valuable than coins."

This whole day, I realized, had been an opportunity to enact this offering. How quickly we forget. With the push for corrective action demanded by my remembrance, I sat down. The Commissioner, a practical man more interested in preventing break-ins than in enlightenment, looked at me in an effort to properly pigeonhole me. He asked where I was from and why I had come to India. My explanation that I had come to stay at the ashram dumbfounded him far more than my coming to his office for Xeroxing.

"And what do you do at the ashram?"

"Pray and meditate, "I said.

"You mean you came *all the way* to India to *pray?*" he said, his impassive face now scrunched in astonishment.

"Yes," I said.

"Don't they have these meditation things in America?"

"Yes," I said. In vain, I searched for words to explain. As he looked at me with his beefy jowls and befuddled look, I was speechless. In a flash, I saw the world through his eyes.

His astonishment reminded me of my first morning in Cairo in a hotel dining room. While I was having breakfast, I marveled at the exotic women with covered heads and floor-length garments. As I was enjoying the spectacle, one of the Egyptian women with a veil on her head approached my table to take a snapshot of my brazen, hoary head. Clearly, I was as exotic to her as she was to me. Part of the cracking of the ego must be the protracted realization that all points of view are just that.

"What *am* I doing here?" I thought. I crossed half the globe to meditate in a country where the pervasive lack of hygiene created more stress than could possibly be removed by the meditation I was doing.

At home, in the States, I lived in exquisite comfort. In our meditation community, we had our own temple-like sanctuary, for which I give thanks to Maharishi. He recognized the growing delicateness of meditators' nervous systems and the need for a natural, protected environment in which to culture this developing refinement. Thus, he called for the establishment of Ideal Villages, or communities. He called for them to be places where the intelligence of nature is lively and where there is freedom from noise. There, surrounded by nature in all her glory, meditators could live and support one another in their spiritual development. These villages were to include a communal building for groups to practice meditation and the TM-Siddhi program. This group practice augments the powerful individual effects of meditation and radiates them out to the world to bring peace.

The Police Commissioner's request for an explanation for my travelling so far to pray and meditate created a mental logjam. Fortunately, the clerk who had managed to prolong the Xeroxing of one page into a twenty-minute ordeal arrived to break it. I thanked them for the copy and made a quick exit.

When I returned to the bank an exhausted-looking Westerner sat by the desk. The clerk motioned me to approach. When the foreigner saw my Xerox, she said with awe, "How did you *get* that?"

I explained.

"I don't know if we'll ever be able to change our traveler's checks," she said. "For almost two hours my husband has been wandering up and down this street trying to get a Xerox copy."

I arrived at the ashram in time to practice my *tabla* before my last lesson that evening. I had gotten money from the bank to give Manju for my lessons. We had never discussed a fee, but I asked around and sensed an amount that would be appropriate. It was late when he finished playing with Swamiji and we started our lesson. Manju agreed to record some *tabla* exercises for me to have at home. We began going through each lesson, a time-consuming process. Manju was a paragon of patience and steadfastness. His focus did not waiver. He showed no signs of fatigue as we neared the third hour of our meeting. It was nearly midnight. Manju was determined to provide me all the tools I needed to continue progressing with my *tabla* playing. In contrast to him, my mind was a sieve, my energy sapped. The slight deviation from my usual bedtime sent my equilibrium lurching.

Over the course of our classes, my affection and respect for Manju had grown. He was pure gold, a noble soul on the planet. Although I had mixed feelings toward Swamiji, I kept appreciating him more through the caliber of his devotee, Manju. When we finally completed the extensive taping, he said,

"Is there anything else, any questions?"

I asked about the mechanics of tuning the *tabla*. He explained. Then I handed him what I hoped was a generous amount of money. He received it easily and with obvious detachment. Looking to the stack of bills in his hand and then to me he said, "This money will be gone in a few days. But what I taught you, you will have for a lifetime."

During our time together, using few words, we communicated with crystal clarity. Through the treasure of music, we bridged two cultures. Manju's grandfather taught his son who, in turn, became Manju's teacher. Manju had taught his own sons, and was now teaching me. This noble pursuit of music passed down through generations now included me. I felt honored.

"I have something for you," Manju said.

I pushed away the hand he extended toward me. It held a small box.

"No, you shouldn't be giving me anything," I said.

It was clearly a reversal of roles. The student should honor the teacher.

"Open it," he said. He was smiling.

I opened the carefully wrapped box. Tears blurred the exquisitely detailed carving of Ganesh.

"Always pray Ganesh," Manju said. "Before playing *tabla*, always pray Ganesh."

"I will," I said. "Thank you. It's beautiful." In Mysore, I'd been in many shops looking at wood carvings but had never seen anything of this quality. Like the caliber of Manju's playing, like the caliber of his soul, the carving was of the highest art.

"And look," he said. He turned the statue upside down. He had taped his card to the bottom of the carving. "This is so you will never forget me. It has my name and address." On the card, he had written, "With best compliments, Manju."

CHAPTER 19

Teaching through Gentleness Is Another Way

*M**other's love is soft. Father's love is strict.*
So, too, is the love of the Divine Mother and Father.

Swamiji sat in the arched window as he did each morning after *puja*. Devotees lined up along the wall separating them from Swamiji and walked past the elevated aperture to receive his blessings. I wondered if the window passing would be any more eventful than the past thirty mornings. He had only spoken to me once, after calling all the angels to the window. I had been excited and felt special. When we arrived, he fiercely told us it was our duty to contribute money for the purchase of headsets for hearing simultaneous translations of Swamiji's talks. I was disappointed, especially with the tone and the word "duty." This was no soft appeal to the heart.

This was my last morning, my last *Sri Chakra Puja,* and my last time to see Swamiji. I stood in the same spot where I had felt so slighted when Swamiji had angrily turned his back once before when I had spoken. Two Russians who shared the dorm room with me in Angel Hall stood right in front of me. This was also their last day. Swamiji smiled and handed them silver medallions bordered in gold. They were effusively overwhelmed. In retrospect, I think Swamiji may have manifested the medallions from thin air. He chatted affectionately with them. Clearly, Swamiji knew this was also my last day. When I approached, he turned his head away but not without an almost furtive glance at me. It seemed to say, "I'm not ignoring you completely, but this is as much as I'm going to give." I was broken-hearted, fed up, and glad I was leaving.

"He's not my guru," I thought. This time he had failed *my* test, the criterion of which was still warm, attentive interaction.

The taxi arrived to take me to Bangalore. Balu, who delivered my carefully folded laundry each week, mysteriously appeared to help me with my luggage. As I was leaving the ashram, I asked the cab driver to stop at the Ayurvedic hospital. I ran in to put more money in the contribution box. When I arrived in Bangalore four hours later, I realized I had miscalculated my funds. I was determined to have a consultation with Swamiji's astrologer in Bangalore. If I had the consultation the next morning as planned, I would barely have enough money to get to the airport. I considered foregoing the astrologer but opted instead, to forgo food.

The modest hotel was an adventure. After weeks in a dormitory, I was all alone in a room. I loved the solitude. Being free from the quiet intensity of the ashram that was slow-cooking me twenty-four hours a day was a relief. Beneath a veneer of propriety, I realized that I was on the verge of screaming much of the time I was there. The television in the room offered novelty, both because it was Indian programming and because I had not seen television for over a month. I realized the world beyond India could have ended, and I would not have known. I turned it on and found a news station. There were riots in New Delhi. Groups of people stormed a movie theater with rocks because

it showed a movie about lesbians. The Hindu party was protesting
with placards, and the theater had pulled the film, fearing rioters would
set the building on fire. I mused about the bland response similar fare
would elicit in the States.

The hotel bathroom was like something from Saturday Night Live.
Pipes came out of the walls with no attachments. Some metal pipes
had connecting portions made from ill-fitting rubber hoses which
yielded fine vertical sprays of water at the junctions. There was a drain
in the middle of the floor to catch water excesses amply supplied from
all directions.

Karunamayi's assistant advised me to take a taxi to the temple.
Amma would be giving *darshan* from seven to nine o'clock that night.
Because I was so low on cash, I decided to go on foot. Walking alone
at night through a large unfamiliar city in a foreign country made me
apprehensive, but it turned out to be an easy jaunt. Bangalore is considered a somewhat liberal, relatively *avant-garde* city. With its book-
stores, something I had never seen in Mysore, it reminded me of an
Indian version of Greenwich Village in New York. A bearded, con-
templative soul sat at the cash register reading in one of the book-
stores. Posters announced lectures and musical events. He spoke English and knew immediately where Karunamayi's temple was. He
stepped out onto the sidewalk to direct me.

I followed the brown brick road up a steep hill and spied the temple
off to the side. I climbed the steps, left my shoes at the door, and
entered a room with a high ceiling. A large gold statue of Saraswati sat
at the front of the hall. The Goddess of Wisdom and Music held her
characteristic lute and smiled benevolently. Off to the left was a throne-
like chair on an elevated platform.

Seated on the floor were about fifteen Indian women in saris. Together they chanted names of Mother Divine in Sanskrit. Although I
tried to join the group inconspicuously, my Westerness made me stand
out like a sore thumb. Even seated, I towered above the other people.
Still not having mastered the art of cross-legged sitting I shifted position every few minutes to find a zone of comfort. Like the statue

before them, the Indian women were still. The temple was simple, a single structure unlike the several buildings forming a compound at the ashram in Mysore.

The temple filled over the next forty minutes, and available spots on the floor began to disappear. Karunamayi entered wearing a red and gold sari, a striking backdrop for her ebony hair. The crowd stood with hands clasped upright in prayer position. Karunamayi smiled, looking carefully from person to person. When she sat, the throne-like chair almost dwarfed her. The majesty of the seat was almost out of place against her softness and humility. A swami, her cousin whom she refers to as her brother, accompanies her on her travels. He stood and, in perfect English, described her recent visit to an ancient temple where she talked of the deities. She had described aspects of the gods depicted in statues and of worship in the ancient culture, astonishing archaeologists and art historians alike.

Karunamayi deferred to people in her entourage to speak, saying only a few words herself. When she did speak I sensed that she was talking directly to me.

"When you first come to India some people say everything is dirty. It is important to look beyond the externals to the rich spirituality behind things."

Karunamayi invited us up for *darshan*. She placed her hand on each person's head and said a few words. I noticed her smiling at me several times when I was sitting. I thought she recognized me from Houston a few months before, but I wasn't sure.

When I went up she said, "Hell-o, Mi-chel. I'm *so* happy to see you again."

After everyone had received *darshan* she stood to leave. I was sorry that she had deferred so much to others to do the talking. As she was moving to leave the hall, she seemed pulled, like a mother who finds it difficult to leave her children. She said, "I love you, Children." She turned and took a step away but, then, looked back. "I love you." Turning back again, she sat down on the step leading to the platform. Everyone scurried toward her to become a small concentrated mass, like a brood of geese nestled around their mother. Arms and legs overlapped as the spaces previously separating people vanished.

Sitting on the step, "Amma," or "Mother," as she is affectionately called, told a story in Telugu. I wished that I had learned to speak some Telugu before I came to India. A man later interpreted it for me.

"Once there was a very holy man, an enlightened *sanyasi* who wandered with only his begging bowl. He knocked on the doors of people's houses to ask for food. At one door a house cleaner answered. She was disgusted and furious, bothered by the beggar's intrusion. She sent him away and slammed the door. He came back several times. Each time she became angrier and screamed at him to go away. Finally, he knocked on the door while she was cleaning. She had some oily rags in her hand. In disgust, she threw the rags at the *sanyasi*. He gathered up the rags. He made 200 wicks for oil lamps from the rags. He distributed these, thereby providing light for 200 people. The washer woman was born the next lifetime into a very wealthy family. This was a result of her good *karma* from giving to the saint, in the form of throwing rags at him. So, it is a very great blessing to be in the company of a realized person. During your lifetime you may never fully understand how great a blessing and how great the benefits are that come from association with a God-realized soul."

After finishing the story, Karunamayi again gave *darshan*. She sprinkled holy water on each person and, using a small brass spoon, ladled a small amount of water into the cupped hands of each person. I watched others drink the water. It was my last night in India. When I went up, Amma put water in my cupped hand and said, "I love you." After the sternness of Swamiji, her warmth and sweetness were soothing balm. I drank the water, but not without thinking that it would be ironic if, after all my phobic efforts to avoid getting dysentery during the past month, this lapse in the final few hours would be my downfall. Once again, life afforded a choice between faith in God and the ever-analytical mind saying, faith is fine, but don't toss your common sense out the window. I had opted for faith, but I knew that if I got sick I would berate myself for not having used my common sense instead.

I didn't get sick. The blessed water, I later learned, was from ritual washing of *salagrama* stones. Hindus worship these black fossils as embodiments of the god Vishnu. They are similar to *shiva linga* stones, honored as embodiments of Shiva. The *darshan* of the *salagrama* stone grants spiritual liberation and is said to cure any disease.

Afterwards I followed the group down steep stairs to the side of the building. There *prasad*, blessed food, was given to devotees. It consisted of a few spoonfuls of cooked rice served on a leaf, the Indian equivalent of a paper plate. Having had only a piece of fruit all day enhanced my gratitude for holy food with Karunamayi's blessing. Divine grace sustained me.

Afterwards I went into the bookstore in the basement of the temple. Much as I loved Karunamayi, the thought of purchasing anything and having to add it to my excessive luggage was an anathema. Although I was short on rupees, I had my check book. I wanted to make a contribution to help support the temple and to show my deep appreciation for Karunamayi. The person behind the counter told me how to make out the check for a contribution, which I did for fifty dollars and gave it to him. It was never cashed. I've often wondered if it was due to some difficulty processing foreign personal checks in India. In truth, I think it was a deliberate message from Karunamayi. She seemed to be saying, "Spirituality is not about money," that my bond with her is unaffected, untainted by money. She seemed to know that I, in particular, needed to know that, especially after what felt like frequent pressure to make donations at the ashram.

CHAPTER 20

Swamiji's Astrologer

The ways of karma are unfathomable.

I awoke with laser-like determination to find Swamiji's astrologer before catching my flight to Germany that afternoon. Years earlier Maharishi had introduced me to *jyotish*, Indian astrology. It has remarkable precision in highlighting future events by dividing one's life into chapters and verses governed by different planets.

Maharishi also introduced me to the remedial measures associated with *jyotish*, whereby Vedic rituals provide a means for "averting the danger that has not yet come." Thus, if an analysis of the *jyotish* chart reveals a problematic upcoming period, the effects can be mitigated by arranging for the appropriate *puja* or *yagya*.

Trained Indian *pandits* recite these Sanskrit rituals to honor and appease the gods and planets who are in charge of the "danger." The Vedic rituals are considered as precise as a chemistry experiment, which must yield the designated result.

104

I was eager to learn what I could from a real *jyotishi*. The hotel clerk delegated the task of helping me use the dreaded Indian telephones to a young boy. He disappeared around the corner with the piece of paper containing the astrologer's phone nu mber. When he was gone for fifteen minutes, I felt my impatience mounting. The time until my plane left was dwindling. Unfortunately, I remembered I had offered my impatience to Swamiji and decided this was yet another opportunity to enact my offering.

When the boy still did not appear, I walked around the corner and found him. He and another child were quizzically pouring through a phone book. I looked at them sitting on the floor I had the distinct impression that they might not know how to read. They explained, in dialect supplemented with gestures, that the phone number I gave them was not valid. I took the phone book and tried to make sense of it myself to no avail. Suddenly, almost as though the decision had come from without, I determined to jump in a cab and simply find the address, without having made an appointment. The cab driver drove unhurriedly. When he began stopping and asking person after person, separated by a few blocks of driving, I gathered that he was almost as unfamiliar with Bangalore as I was.

After another thirty minutes, we inched down a narrow street and stopped before a humble dwelling. I asked him to wait until I was sure the astrologer was, indeed, there. A woman with a puzzled look on her face greeted me. She spoke no English, and I spoke not a word of her dialect. She looked at the paper with the astrologer's name and let loose with a flood of incomprehensible words. The taxi driver got out and talked to her. They began pointing in different directions. It was clear that our journey was not over. The driver explained that the astrologer had moved. The woman knew approximately where he lived but did not have an exact address. Back in the cab, I now came to appreciate fully the value of my driver's patience. He did not seem in the slightest bit put off by the task of delivering me to a person whose address we did not have. We drove in circles, met half the people in the neighborhood, and through some miracle eventually arrived at the astrologer's house.

Doubtful, I again asked the driver to wait. When an Indian woman opened the door, and I spotted a large pink photograph of Swamiji, I knew we were at the right place. The woman, who did not speak English, warmly embraced me as though I were a long-lost daughter. A few minutes later a spry, energetic man in his eighties came to the door. He spoke perfect English, but his accent was so thick that I had difficulty understanding him.

"I'm eating, I'm eating," he said. "You'll have to wait. Come in. Come in." He was clearly thinking much faster than I was. He looked out at the taxi and shooed him away with gestures.

"I think I should have him wait," I said.

"No, no, no," he said. "There are hundreds of taxis around here."

Wondering if I was sending away my link to Germany, I paid the taxi and said good-bye.

I waited in a small room, rather amazed that against all odds I was apparently about to have my *jyotish* reading. The kind woman who greeted me returned with tea and two small plates of food I could not identify. She urged me to eat. I was at a loss as to the proper combining or sequencing of the two foods. A young man in his twenties who spoke flawless English came in and sat at a computer. He asked for my birth information. He fed it to the computer, which in turn spat out several pages of data.

"Uncle will be in shortly to give your consultation." He looked at the printed pages with a furrowed brow. Although his was a quieter brand, I could see intensity ran in the family. I asked questions showing some technical knowledge of Indian astrology.

"From what you're saying and from your chart I see you have a facility for *jyotish,*" he said. He pointed out the configuration of planet indicating this.

"So you do readings, too," I said.

"I'm in training with uncle. I'm his apprentice. He's seventy-nine now, so he's training me to take over one day."

He seemed to enjoy spreading his wings and pointed out a few more things in my chart. When his uncle walked into the consultation room, he was quietly reverential. He took a seat in the corner next to another young man, his brother, and observed the master.

"Come, come," his uncle said to me, impatience or efficiency, I wasn't sure which, ringing in his voice. He motioned for me to get up from the chair and follow him to a tiny room, not much bigger than a closet. Inside it were statues of deities, a picture of Swamiji, and a life-size photograph of Sai Baba, the popular Indian saint.

"Kneel down. Pray before the consultation."

He knelt too. The rapidity of movement gave way to a moment of still sacredness barricaded off from the rest of time. I said a prayer. Then we stood up and rushed back to the consultation room. He peered with focused intent at my chart, flipping pages and writing calculations on the sheet.

Finally, he made a pronouncement, as though it were a hopeless situation.

"You are Indian to the core. You are disgusted with material life." On hearing this, his two nephews began howling with laughter. I didn't fully understand, but the laughter was infectious, and I joined in. He delivered each subsequent pronouncement like a blade of truth slicing through the *maya* of illusion. Its freshness resulted in gales of laughter.

"In your last life you were an orthodox *Brahmin* (member of the priestly caste). Your chart indicates *yogabrashta,* the attainment of a high state of yoga in a past life followed by its willful destruction."

We laughed at this tragedy, which I added to my scribbled notes.

"You see, after attaining great spiritual powers and a high *Brahmin* level, you fell in love with an American man. This may have occurred here in Bangalore," he said, "because 15,000 American troops were in the state of Karnataka beginning in 1940. You had a desire for comforts and pleasure. It was due to this *karma* of dying with these desires unfulfilled that you were born in the U.S."

For some reason, everyone, including myself, found this notion hilarious. It was as if my Indian brothers and I just reunited, and we were laughing at the preposterous events that had led to our separation.

"In the first half of your Venus period you were married. You wanted to fulfill desires for sex and material comforts. You were comfortable, although you can be comfortable without material things. Fulfillment of desires, however, did not offer full satisfaction because spirituality was obstructing."

Again we laughed. Often he made his pronouncements with such a heavy accent that I would have to wait until the nephews recovered their composure to interpret. They all watched me like a hawk. When my eyes indicated that I understood, a second round of laughter ensued, this time including me.

"It was your past life *poonya*, or good deeds, that did not allow you to obtain full satisfaction of enjoyment from material comforts," he said. "Between 1988 and 1991 you were going this way and that between spirituality and material life—whether to be a philosopher or whether to be married again. You could not decide on your own. Fortunately, you did not find a man to your taste. Although it looks unfortunate, it is actually fortunate as I will explain later when we discuss your destiny."

The uncle had been a lawyer with the Indian government before he turned to astrology. He has been Swamiji's astrologer for nearly twenty years. He foretold his world travels before Swamiji had even learned English. Swamiji raised the astrologer's nephews in the ashram. From childhood they learned to perform Sanskrit rituals and to chant the Vedas.

"You have an ability to be a master musician or artist in any of the fine arts. Your financial future is bright, indicated by Jupiter's aspect on the moon and ascendant. This *gajakesuri* configuration shows you are destined to maintain elephants and lions." I furiously wrote this down and then realized it made no sense to me.

"I'll have elephants and lions?" I said.

They all laughed. This time I didn't join in. I was too busy trying to understand.

"This doesn't mean you will own a zoo," the nephew said. "It's language from the time when kings maintained elephants and lions. It means you will be very comfortable. Having lions and elephants is like having a BMW." He laughed again.

"The purpose of your life," the uncle said, "is to have partial enjoyment through sex with Americans. During the rest of your life, however, the commission of your life is different. The horoscope is splendid. From now on you will desire more for the elevation of your soul and for *puja* and prayers. There is abundant *poonya*, past life credit. Your original *poonya* will force you to fulfill your spiritual longing. It will allow nothing less. The chart indicates that it is God's will that you must lead a saintly, *sanyasi* life, helping the downtrodden. Then only, do you get satisfaction. Like Swamiji, you help the downtrodden. You have the same ascendant, Taurus, as Swamiji. This explains the magnetic attraction between you."

I hardly felt that a "magnetic attraction" characterized my recent experience with Swamiji, but I was silent on this point. As I was rushing to the airport, I realized that this meeting was the only light-hearted time I had had during my month in India.

At the airport all ten computers for checking people in crashed simultaneously. Long, stagnant lines froze before hapless clerks who, with a single finger, hit non-responsive lone keys on the computer.

When the Lufthansa flight was finally in the air, my being heaved a sigh of relief. During my stay I wondered with horror whether I could adapt if some cataclysm forced me to live the rest of my life in India. I doubted that I could. I might be "Indian to the core," but it was clear that whatever longing led to my being reborn in the West is still deeply embedded in my cells.

CHAPTER 21

Leave Me Alone–I'm Happy

Whenever we penetrate the heart of things we find a mystery.
— Albert Schweitzer

Back in the States I noticed an ambivalence toward Swamiji. I still had pictures of him around the house but avoided making eye contact with them. More than ever, I appreciated his power and feared that any opening on my part would lead to extreme vulnerability again.

My adopted daughter Vera knows me very well. She could see beyond my dread to the good that Swamiji was doing me. She had trained as a physician but later decided to give it up. Her diagnostic ability blends with her newly open third eye—the area between the eyebrows activated by transmission of spiritual energy. When opened, it gives clear vision of the truth beyond appearances. Third eye vision often transcends limitations of space and time so that she can see future events. Before I went to India, I had given Vera a picture of Swamiji. She accurately perceived a great deal about him from his photograph, and, so, without having met him she knew him well.

"He's protecting you. I think he's helping you. I like his strictness," she said. Her Greek accent added authenticity to her perception, as though the Oracle of Delphi had spoken.

Her certainty contrasted with my cowering.

—◀⧓▶—

Life after India was gentle. My appreciation of creature comforts had became stronger. I extended my leave of absence from work and eased into a slow pace. My body dictated my tempo, a rhythm that felt in tune with the unhurried changes of nature. I did what I wanted when I wanted, writing and playing the piano, framed by morning and evening meditation.

Later, news that Karunamayi was visiting the U.S. penetrated my cherished solitude. I was eager to see her again. I wanted to re-establish my personal link with the saintly energies of India without arousing fear.

At one of her first meetings in the United States she had said, "I have seen you in India, and I have come all this way only to be with you. I have not come to you as Guru. I have never wanted the post of Guru. I have not come to you as a God. But I have come to you as your own mother."

—◀⧓▶—

On the day of Karunamayi's visit in Dallas, Vera and I arrived early to obtain front seats. A cardiologist visiting from Iran named Tanas joined us. We planted our belongings in the front row and walked over to the bookstall. A young man dressed in white with a bright, open face recruited us into service. Our *seva* (service) consisted of sitting on the floor to count audio cassettes of Karunamayi chanting mantras. The elevating sound of her soft, high-pitched voice filled the room. Keeping the volume of her chanting low over the next two days showed respect for our delicate physiologies, sensitized by her presence.

Sitting with Karunamayi, I felt gently blissful. I wanted to be no place else; I wanted nothing more. While waiting our turn for private meetings with her, Tanas, Vera, and I brainstormed about starting a business.

"We have to be able to work in our nightgowns at home, preferably in bed. That's the number-one requirement. I think it should be an internet business," Vera said.

"Let's start a *Karma* Travel Agency," I said. "It would send people to different destinations based on their merit."

We giggled.

"People could never complain." Tanas said. "Horrible roach-infested hotels or flights canceled would never be a problem. The business could not fail because if customers complained, we would just say, 'It's your *karma*. Sorry, there's nothing we can do about it.'"

Our silliness had a childlike quality to it that seemed fitting in the presence of our divine mother.

We quelled our giggling when the Swami accompanying Karunamayi walked to the microphone.

"As a special blessing Amma has brought from India some rare *salagrama* stones. These fossils come from a special Himalayan stream. The stones represent the power of Vishnu. Sipping water that has washed salagrama stones will instantaneously purify even the worst criminal. When you come up to meet with Amma, you will receive *darshan* and some of the holy water. Cup your hands and drink the water."

When it was my turn to go up, I approached, and Karunamayi said, "Hello Mi-chel."

I was touched that she called me by name as she had in India. She asked about my work.

"You are a very good psychologist," she said.

Her face became animated when I asked her to bless my piano playing and writing. She took my hands in hers. She turned them from side to side, looking at them.

"You are Saraswati," she said. I felt inspired as she identified me with the Indian Goddess of the Arts. In fact, she was simply reminding me that we are all one with the divine, that the self and the Self are one.

Vera's turn: dressed in a beige suit, she went up and sat in the yellow overstuffed armchair facing Karunamayi. When she returned, Vera said, "I told her I'm having problems with my husband and that I feel very lonely."

"Karunamayi said, 'You're not alone. There are 20,000 souls surrounding you and protecting you.'"

"I love that image," I said. "It's a wonderful one to call to mind."

CHAPTER 22

The Hugging Saint

You are prone to love as the sun is to shine;
it being the most delightful and natural employment of the soul
of man.

— Thomas Traherne

Many Indian saints do not touch, but Ammachi does. She had been giving love for hours, since early morning. She has kissed faces, sprinkled pastel flower petals on hair, wiped away tears with her shawl, tousled hair, laughingly put rose petals in ears, and folded people's palms around Hershey's candy kisses. This is her unique method of giving *darshan*, transmitting spiritual energy to those in immediate contact. She would continue until four the next morning, then board a plane to repeat the process yet again in another city on her world tour.

While Ammachi was busy giving love in Dallas, I was *en route* from Austin to see her. I drove with Irene, the girlfriend of Christopher, an Ammachi devotee I had met previously. Christopher had been on the straight and narrow, a member of the Church of Christ until he felt like a pressure cooker about to explode from endless rules and escalating guilt. This ultimately led to his ejection into unbounded realms where he landed upon Hinduism. In Ammachi's saintly presence, he felt he had found a living embodiment of Christ's selfless love and healing. His deep appreciation of the Christ energy was very congruent with his Christ-like appearance: shoulder length hair; languid, tall body; and compassionate expression. His girlfriend, Irene, was petite, blond, and bubbly. He invited her to see Ammachi, who was to be her introduction to Hinduism.

Irene had an openness and directness about her that I enjoyed. We'd been talking so intently that the five-hour trip to Dallas seemed like minutes. Soon my soul was smiling as I sat in the *darshan* line approaching Ammachi for a blessing.

Someone once asked, "Don't you get tired sitting giving *darshan* for eighteen, twenty hours at a time?"

"No," Ammachi said. "Where there is true love there is no effort."

Touching the feet of a saint destroys all sins and confers immeasurable benefits. At the Ammachi gathering, a devotee holding the saint's sandals stopped in front of me. Indian scriptures say that Divine energy enters the top of the head of the guru and leaves through the feet. By worshiping the feet, one worships the Supreme Truth manifested as the guru. "Would you like to touch Ammachi's sandals?" he said. I bowed my head and touched them.

"You know," he said, "the guru's sandals are considered even more sacred than the guru's feet."

"The sandals are more sacred than the feet?" I said. This seemed inconceivable. "Why?" I said.

"Because the sandals link the guru with the earth. They remind us of the guru's decision to incarnate to help mankind."

To date, the logic is unclear to me. It seems that feet are a more necessary link than sandals. However, what do I, who incarnated in New Jersey of all places, know of such things?

In India, sometimes groups of several thousands gather to see Ammachi. People may wait for eight to ten hours for her *darshan*. In

Dallas the line of seated people awaiting Ammachi unhurriedly snaked toward her. I crossed my legs. I was in the familiar yet uncomfortable floor-sitting pose linked to my spiritual path. I scooted forward every five minutes or so as the line slowly moved closer to Ammachi's radiant light. A long purple silk scarf was draped around my shoulders. My efforts to toss the ends with a flamboyant flair alternated with my becoming entangled, practically strangling myself with it while sliding forward on the floor. I waved across the large room to Christopher and Irene who stood with arms laced around each other's backs. Christopher looked blissful and delighted with the setting. Irene looked less convinced.

A bright-eyed Indian man sitting in front of me turned around. His face was like a sunflower in full bloom.

"I've seen you before," he said.

"You do look familiar," I said, "but, I'm not sure where we met. Could it have been with Ammachi last year?"

"No, this is the first time I've come to see her," he said.

"Oh, you're in for a treat then. Wait till you receive *darshan*."

"I think I know where I saw you. Did you go to see Karunamayi a few weeks ago?"

"Yes. That's where it was," I said. "Isn't Karunamayi wonderful?"

"I have to tell you what happened. I'm the chair of the Telugu Association in Dallas. Since Karunamayi speaks Telugu I helped host her visit. The night before I was to drive her to the airport Karunamayi appeared to me in a dream. She said, 'Come at five o'clock tomorrow morning to do *Pada Puja*. And don't forget to bring the milk.' [She was referring to the Vedic ceremony to honor and receive blessings from the feet of the guru, a tradition that spans many spiritual paths. In Biblical times, for example, Mary Magdalene anointed the feet of Christ.]

"At four in the morning, I woke up, and although I never get up that early, I was wide-awake. I started to get dressed, and my wife woke up.

"'What are you doing?' she said.

"'I have to go to our friend's house to do *puja*.'

"'Are you crazy?' she said. 'It's four o'clock in the morning.'

"I just told her, 'I have to go.'

"So, I grabbed a bottle of milk from the refrigerator and drove to my friend's house. It was about five in the morning when I got there. My friend came to the door in his pajamas, his eyes half-closed.

"'What are you doing here so early? Go and sleep in the living room. We'll wake you up before seven to go to the airport.'

"Just then his wife came down the stairs and said, 'Karunamayi wants to do *Pada Puja* now.'

"'We can't. We don't have any milk for the ceremony,' my friend said.

"'I brought the milk,' I said. I didn't explain to them that Karunamayi appeared to me in a dream and told me to bring the milk.

"Karunamayi arrived in a red sari. 'So, is everyone ready?' she said.

"There wasn't any commotion yet in the outer world. It was such a holy moment, to be present with a saint in the pre-dawn hours doing *puja*. We chanted the Sanskrit words, and tears started coming down my face."

His story had a familiar, magical ring to it.

"Are those kinds of amazing coincidences the norm for Indians?" I said. "I met an Indian woman who told me story after story like that, of gurus appearing in dreams. In fact, she told me about another Indian saint you might know. He speaks Telugu, too. Have you heard of Swamiji?"

His face lit up.

"Yes," he said. "I saw him last year in Louisiana."

"I saw him there, too," I said. "That's why you look so familiar. We keep seeing each other when we go to see different saints."

"That's another amazing story," he said. "A woman asked me to put a notice in our Telugu Association newsletter. She wanted to Federal Express the notice because the newsletter was already in press. I said O.K. The red and white envelope arrived the next day, and I hand-delivered it to the printer. When I opened it, I saw this picture of Swamiji. I was struck. I read the notice about his visit to Louisiana. I called the woman who sent me the announcement and asked if I could keep the photograph of Swamiji. That photograph was on my desk, and something about Swamiji just kept growing on me.

"I had a business conference scheduled in Ohio the weekend Swamiji was to arrive in Louisiana from India. I had plane tickets and hotel reservations. The Friday I was supposed to leave, I said to my wife, 'I'm not going to Ohio. We're going to Louisiana for the weekend to meet Swamiji.'

"We drove about thirteen hours. It was the weekend of *Guru Poornima*. I wanted so much to stay for the *Pada Puja* ceremony on Sunday, but I had to get back to Dallas. I stood to leave, feeling disappointed, and I went outside. Swamiji was just entering the building. There was a crowd around him. He had never met me before. He had no way of knowing I was from Dallas. I don't think he's ever been there, in fact. He looked right at me. Then he walked over to me and took off his pink scarf. He handed it to me and said, 'I'll see you in Dallas.' It was mind-boggling. And now, it turns out, he's coming to Dallas this year!"

"I hate to tell you this," I said. "His trip to the States is canceled. I got a newsletter from the temple in Louisiana. Because the world situation is so tenuous Swamiji canceled his trip. He's staying at the ashram in India to do *pujas*. In fact, the newsletter said it's by divine decree that he's doing the *pujas*."

"It *was* canceled," my Indian friend said, a smile spreading across his face. "But there's been a change. Swamiji is going to make a surprise visit to the U.S."

Excitement and terror shot through me.

"When?" I said.

"The dates haven't been set yet. If you give me your phone number, I'll let you know. It will be within the next couple of months."

Vera strolled barefoot over from the bookstand, her white linen dress brushing the floor. She sat down beside me in the *darshan* line.

"This is Vera," I said. "What is your name?"

I realized we'd been talking like old friends yet hadn't exchanged names.

"I'm R.K.," he said. "Like O.K., but with an R."

"And I'm Michael."

Vera looked at him, and an expression of certainty came over her face.

"I know you," she said. "I usually don't recognize people, but you stood out. You were at Karunamayi's, weren't you?"

"Yes," he said.

"R.K. just told me that Swamiji is coming," I said.

"Oh, my God. When?" She turned to me. "I'm going to have to take you to him."

In a split second she saw her role and responsibility as a loving daughter. She would lead me by the hand to this difficult medicine. On my own I would likely have avoided it, even though my life had improved since I returned from India. My feelings of compassion had grown, encompassing people for whom I would have felt only judgment. My intuition had become uncannily accurate and came back to bite me when I didn't follow it. The sudden crashing of a plant or news that I had avoided a very negative meeting showed me that my intuition was not to be ignored. Time spent alone was more fulfilling, and times with people more enjoyable because of greater warmth and friendliness.

Over the next hour and a half of scooting forward on the long red carpet, the line advanced, and the intensity of Ammachi's aura grew stronger. We were now just a few feet from her. I could feel myself progressively dispersing into disconnected particles of matter. R.K. was ahead of us. Ammachi reached out and put her arms around him, and he disappeared into the ocean of her bliss.

I now sat right in front of Ammachi. Rhythmic devotional songs blasted through the loud speakers. Warm flesh pressed in on all sides from those packed in closely around me. When it was my turn, white-clothed attendants with hands on my back pushed me toward her. Instantly I was gone—lost in her divine embrace. Like the times before, I was caught up in a huge wave, being turned upside down. My eyes were closed. Ammachi whispered, "Ma, ma, ma, ma," into my ear. The power from those simple syllables ripped me loose from my usual boundaries. Disoriented, I lost all bearings, like a child caught in an undertow and spun around underwater in an ocean wave. From my usual stance of separateness watching the powerful river of life flow past me, here I was swept into and becoming one with the river. My mind dissolved into pure feeling as my heart poured into Amma's heart.

This experience with Ammachi was familiar to me. I did not resist it. It was an experience of going beyond stale and constricted emotional patterns. It was fresh, like the roaring sea.

Gently tugged and directed by attendants I stood up in a daze and precariously found my way to the nearby "resting chair." Grateful to be able to land, I sat to absorb the experience.

When my amorphous mind regained its ability to shape words, I heard the voice of my soul: "This is the answer."

The phrase echoed in my head for about fifteen minutes. Then, with absolute innocence I began to weep. It was a cleansing without name. It was not sadness, nor joy, nor any identifiable feeling—just a dam unleashed through gates flown open.

Someone once asked Ammachi what the role of the intellect was on the spiritual path.

"To be destroyed," she said. "The mind divides. The heart unites."

Ammachi's unconditional love is God's love for us flowing through her. Teaching by example, she embodies the divine. One of her Indian devotees described his search for a guru:

I anticipated that a guru must perform miracles. By showing power over the laws of nature, a true guru would prove his divinity to me. So, with this test in mind, I traveled around India in search of my guru. When I got to the small village where Ammachi lived, she was giving *darshan* in a small hut. It was very hot with no air condition-ing or fan. A long line of people stood waiting. Then a leper came into the hut. The stench was so horrible that some people actually fainted. When he went up to Ammachi, however, she reached out her arms and embraced him as though greeting a long-lost son who had come home. She hugged him and kissed his face. Then she began to lick his wounds. It was then, in seeing her absolute unconditional love, that I knew I had found my guru. What I witnessed was not the flashy kind of miracle I thought I wanted. I witnessed the miracle of divine love and knew I had found what I was seeking.

Sitting in the presence of Ammachi, I realized no part of my being resisted her. There was no fear. I felt expanded and renewed. I had no concerns about materialism somehow sullying her or her organization. There was no hierarchy, no elitism. She embraced all, literally and figuratively. Every cell of her body, every moment of her being was spent in giving. Whenever I see her I feel as though all parts of myself are put back into perspective; my values, to the extent that they had deviated from a position of altruism, are re-aligned.

CHAPTER 23

Avoiding the Inevitable

*If you do not change direction, you may
end up where you are heading.*

— Lao-tzu

A few weeks later Vera and I drove through a maze of flashing lights and sideswiping cars in Dallas.

"Have you heard any news yet about when Swamiji is coming?" Before she could answer, I continued, "I don't know why I'm so anxious to get the dates of his visit. I'm really terrified to see him, but he's driving me crazy. I want to figure out what is going on."

"Why are you so terrified? I like Swamiji. To me he's *Shiva*," she said, referring to the Indian god who destroys anything that binds.

"He *is* *Shiva*, and he's intolerant of my ways. I don't think he likes me."

"HE *ADORES* YOU."

The tone was emphatic and the voice a couple of octaves lower than usual, booming as she stretched out the words. The assertive tone was antithetical to any sympathizing with my feelings, and the dogmatic flavor did not allow for rebuttal. I was silent and perplexed, unconvinced and feeling abandoned. After a few minutes Vera's high-pitched voice reappeared with the rapid pace of her usual speech.

"And that *wasn't* me talking!" she said.

We started laughing at this obvious truth.

"That was so weird," I said. "All of a sudden you were completely gone. I felt like I was in the car with a stranger."

Some weeks later, I said to Vera, "I've been thinking, even if Swamiji *does* come to the States, I don't think I'm going to see him."

"YOU *HAVE* TO SEE HIM." Her voice was deep and thundering. Then she said, "That was him talking again."

We laughed. I stopped entertaining the notion of not going to see Swamiji.

"Don't worry. Your daughter is going to take her mom to see Swamiji."

Vera's certainty was puzzling.

"Why are you so sure about Swamiji being good for me?" I asked.

"Because he's teaching you the last lessons. These are the final lessons you need to learn before you become enlightened. It's all about the conflict with your father and your fears about men. Through Swamiji, you will get beyond it."

Impatient now, I called the Swamiji center in Mississippi a few days later. Rao answered the phone.

"Swamiji's visit has been finalized," he said. He provided dates and recommended hotels in Louisiana.

"I heard Swamiji is going to be in Dallas, too," I said. "It's closer so I'd prefer going there. Will there be a program in Dallas?"

"No. Swamiji is going to be in Dallas for just a few hours at my daughter's house. He'll meet with some people to discuss upcoming projects. It's not a program open to the public. Swamiji will fly in and out the same day."

"I see," I said. I was disappointed by the convenience that had just been swept out of reach.

Word of Swamiji's impending visit spread. I joined with a group of four among the "goers."

CHAPTER 24

Terror Re-awakened

We must be willing to get rid of the life we've planned, so as to have the life that is awaiting . . . The old skin has to be shed before the new one is to come.

— Joseph Campbell

Christopher, the longhaired, theologically-inclined therapist who discovered Hinduism with a vengeance, was our driver. He wore a light blue denim shirt that matched his eyes. Tall and lanky, his dusty blond hair and peaceful expression gave him an ethereal look. Having been profoundly moved by Ammachi's powerful presence, he decided to see Swamiji in hopes of some more heavenly bliss. Samantha, a meditation teacher who loved to chant the Vedas, also joined us. Like me, she was smitten after seeing a photograph of him. She had a cooler as big as her suitcase filled with organic, non-genetically engineered foods. Her silken grey hair and flawless skin attested to the benefits of her careful diet and daily oil massages. Vera joined us, looking tired

125

from an early morning flight from Dallas. As we set off on our six-hour drive to Baton Rouge, she sprawled out in the back seat, intent on making up for the sleep lost through her dawn departure and her graduate school program.

"All right, here's a rule. No talking until we get to Louisiana," I said, dreading conversation and the strain of civility. I began to meditate. An hour later the no-talking ban started disintegrating.

After some lazy banter, Samantha, always eager to raise the vibration, suggested that we chant some mantras. "How about Karunamayi's homage to Saraswati, *Om ayim srim hrim Saraswati devyai namah?*"

She led, and we followed. The repetitive sounds created a background like Gregorian chant, turning the car into a mobile monastery. It was a divine substitute for yak. This continued over the next few hours as we drifted in and out of silence. As we chanted, I remembered that repetition of this same mantra was the only thing in Mekedatu that had lessened my physical pain.

Once we left Texas behind and crossed the Louisiana state boundary the impending meeting with Swamiji seemed more real, and our sense of expectancy rose.

"Christopher, you've seen Swamiji before, haven't you?" Samantha asked.

"No, this is my first time."

"And how about you, Vera?"

"It's the first time for me, too," she said.

"So, Michael's the only one who's seen him."

"And she went to India to see him. What an experience she had," Vera said.

"What happened in India? Irene told me you said the bathrooms weren't quite like the Holiday Inn, but she didn't go into any detail," Christopher said.

"Well, I don't want to spoil your innocence in seeing Swamiji, so I won't go into it all. But I'll just say that Swamiji is different. He doesn't have that warm, fuzzy, nurturing quality that I'm always seeking."

"He's strict. He's *very* strict," Vera said. "In fact, he could bite your head off. He's very powerful. Oh, is he powerful!"

"How do you know?" Christopher said. "I thought you hadn't seen him yet."

"I just know. Believe me, I know."

"He's definitely unpredictable and very powerful," I said. "I'll tell you a story that will give you a flavor. When I was staying at the ashram there was a special three-day celebration for Lord Dattatreya's birthday. Swamiji is thought to be the incarnation of the three deities, Vishnu, Shiva, and Brahma, as was Lord Dattatreya before him. Anyway, as part of this celebration there was the option of sponsoring different *yagyas*, which can modify *karma* or get some precisely targeted divine help with a particular problem. One listed on the menu was a mega-*yagya* that encompassed all the smaller ones. It was very expensive, but I figured I'd come to India to enhance my spiritual evolution. "If this will help me along, it's worth doing," I thought.

"The next morning I found a spot on a straw mat on the chilly floor in the prayer hall. After morning *puja* and prayers, one of the priests said something in Telugu. My name was embedded in the unfamiliar words. I didn't understand. People started nudging me to go up to the front of the prayer hall. I was completely perplexed. People kept edging me closer until I was right in front of Swamiji. He handed me a scarf, some books, and other gifts. Everyone started applauding. I still hadn't a clue about what was going on. Later I found out that, although I thought I had sponsored a mega-*yagya*, in fact, I had paid for dinner for the whole ashram for a day. I don't know whether this was in addition to the *yagyas* or instead of them.

"I also sponsored some less expensive *yagyas* for the following day. That night, back in the dorm, I was talking to an English woman who asked why I went up to the front and got so much attention from Swamiji. I told her about my inadvertent purchase of dinner for the entire ashram. We started laughing, and I said some very irreverent things about buying greasy rice when I thought I was sponsoring *yagyas*. We had another good laugh and then went to sleep.

"The next morning I went to the appointed place for another yagya I'd sponsored. Part way into the Vedic recitation the priest mentioned those sponsoring the *yagya*. When my name wasn't mentioned, a man next to me said, 'You really should speak up. In order for you to obtain the benefit of the *yagya* the priest has to have you in his consciousness during the recitation.'

"I interrupted the priest. He seemed quite annoyed but indicated that the situation had to be remedied. He stopped the ritual and took me to an office in an adjacent building. They had a computer with all different *yagyas* and the names of the sponsors. The person at the computer didn't have me down for the *yagya* in question. Instead, he had me down as sponsoring another mega-*yagya*/dinner for the whole ashram.

"'There's a mistake,' I said.

"'Well, wouldn't you like to sponsor the mega-*yagya* in addition to the *yagya* this morning?' he asked. (Of course, he didn't call it a mega-*yagya*, but I forget the name.)

"I could feel myself contracting and holding on to my pennies.

"'No, I just did that one yesterday,' I said.

"We clarified that I was sponsoring only the *yagya* in process. We returned to the altar, and the priest continued with the ritual.

"When it was over we joined the large group assembled for morning prayers and *puja* with Swamiji. He almost never spoke in English in India. Occasionally he'd say two or three sentences. However, on this morning he launched into an English diatribe.

"He seemed to have singled me out, and it was clear that he was addressing the six foreigners. He was obviously aware of my irreverent conversation, whispered with the English woman in the dorm room the night before. He seemed to know I was laughing then, too. And, he seemed to know I didn't want to sponsor feeding the ashram again.

"'This ashram is not for Swamiji,' he said. The volume and intensity of his voice rose. 'Swamiji does not need. This ashram exists only for your benefit. So, to support ashram is your duty. When you have money, you give. Otherwise, you are Satan.'

"His eyes were shooting fire, and he was practically shouting.

"'Don't say, 'Yesterday I gave, so today I won't give. Who laughs about giving money for food for the ashram is devil. You are Satan. You are devil.'

"His chastisement went on longer, but that was the essence of it. How he knew about my whispered conversation in the dorm room or my refusal to sponsor a second big yagya, I don't know. I suspect that he has omniscience and the ability to tune into different conversations at different places at a distance. In fact, I'm getting afraid that he's monitoring my telling this story now. We'd better change the subject or I might get into more trouble," I said.

I could feel my terror rising like the hairs on a frightened cat's back. "What ever possessed me to organize this trip to a face-to-face meeting with the source of my dread?" I thought.

I later read that Swamiji has had clairaudience since he was a child. I also learned that following his mother's death when he was a boy, he went from door to door begging for food. Perhaps this is why my joking about the ashram's program that provides free food resulted in such a display of anger.

CHAPTER 25

Reunion

To be at one with God is to be at peace.
— Ralph W. Trine

As soon as we walked into the crowded prayer hall I was blasted by divinity. Melted into an ornate gold chair in the center of the stage was Swamiji. I knew exactly what had possessed me to make the trip to Baton Rouge: it was Swamiji's presence.

We were late and sidled up the seated crowd to the front of the hall. We placed our backjacks at the corner of the stage before the first row of chairs. Not long after we sat down, Swamiji stood up and walked with small, labored steps on elevated wooden sandals. His gait was almost 'Parkinsonian.'

I recalled a remark I heard in India. We were discussing our upcoming private meetings with Swamiji at his ashram when we would have the precious chance to each ask him a question to guide our lives. We were debating among ourselves about what to ask. An English woman, singularly detached from the reverence permeating the ashram, said, "When I have my private audience I'm going to ask, 'Aren't you horribly uncomfortable walking around in those elevated wooden shoes?'"

Swamiji walked across the stage and down the steps. Then he walked over to a couch four feet from us and sat down.

My mind was quiet, but I could not hold onto it. It kept slipping away and fusing with some transcendent reality. I felt myself zooming through other dimensions, and then landing back in my body with a start. Occasionally, I would open my eyes and look at Swamiji. After a brief glimpse, however, I could not resist the desire to close my eyes again. Like looking at the sun, it was too much to bear.

I left conceptual paraphernalia behind. Occasionally a thought would drift like a lonely boat on the ocean of my awareness. In my reverie I heard Swamiji say telepathically, 'You have the gift of traveling through different worlds.' I knew to what he referred. A Native American medicine woman had told me of my travels with her in the spirit world to doctor people.

When I was slightly more grounded I mused about wanting Swamiji's help with eating better and having more energy. This time I heard him convey in a strong, unabashed way, "You have no talent for cooking." He telepathically repeated this several times. The message seemed to be, "You have no talent for cooking. Wake up and face this truth," as if this were the starting point for corrective action. Some weeks later I realized he was recommending that I stop trying to find a solution by cooking, which I detest, and instead, turn to someone with a talent for cooking. That is, I should get a cook.

He eventually "delivered" a magnificent Pakistani cook to me. Remembering his message when I saw a woman in a Punjabi dress at the YMCA back in Texas, I ran up to her and asked if she knew anyone who could prepare Indian meals for me.

"Well, my husband is a very good cook. We used to have a restaurant in California. I'll ask him," she said.

Mohan, her husband, began preparing delectable meals for the meditation community where I live. He prepared delicately spiced mixed vegetables, dal, rice biriyani, golden poori bread, and rice pudding. Perhaps my meeting him was my good *karma* from having purchased dinner for the ashram in Mysore.

As Swamiji, draped in a bright pink sari, sat on the magenta and gold couch, his attendants, in white *dhotis*, set up musical instruments and loud speakers. Various devotees, both Indian and American, came before the couch and bowed to Swamiji. Some offered gifts. He radiated charm and affection as he chatted with them.

Still in my swoon, I glanced up every few minutes. Each time I did so the vision of Swamiji catapulted me right back to my interior silence. Once when I peeked, I saw an American kneeling and talking with him. There was a sense of familiarity between them as if they were seeing each other again after several months. Swamiji's expression was amicable. I shut my eyes and was lost again. I felt my daughter lean toward me and whisper, "Now I understand why you're afraid of Swamiji."

I was incapable of processing the comment or reacting. Absorbing a saint's radiance has no counterpart in words. It is as distinct from everyday reality as swimming is from walking. Near the power of that holy emanation, it is impossible to think and experience at the same time. The usual skittish movement of thoughts on the surface vanishes and gives way to the depth of the ocean and fullness of undivided experience.

Swamiji moved from the couch to the stage and took with him the intensity of radiance he had been beaming toward our little group. What we lost in proximity we later gained in cumulative effects of time spent with him. With the *tabla* rhythm as backdrop, Swamiji joined in with his musicians. He played the synthesizer. He sang. Swamiji's healing music from the spheres soothes and expands. It infuses divine tranquility and is an aid to meditation. Its sublime vibration has cured diseases and brought about emotional healing.

When he sings, his voice is like a clarion of light in the dark *Kaliyuga* age, the last of four phases of time through which the universe cycles. In *Kaliyuga* the forces of ignorance are in full power. It is comparable to the darkest period of the night.

When the concert ended, a chubby Indian man walked up to the microphone. He was Radhakrishna, who has been with Swamiji since he was a boy and who frequently travels with him on his world tours. "Lunch will be served here tomorrow at noon, but the program for the general public will not begin until *six o'clock* tomorrow night. During the day Swamiji will meet with those individuals sponsoring audiences."

Samantha leaned toward me and whispered, "How much is it to sponsor an audience?"

"I don't know." I was still in an expanded state of consciousness, far from discrete facts and information.

She checked with some people sitting nearby. She turned to me again. "Well, nix that. It's five hundred dollars."

The crowd stood up, hands folded at their chests in prayer position. Swamiji walked out of the hall. We followed in silence heading for the car. Knowing that our able and grounded driver-companion Christopher would deliver us to the hotel, we could maintain our expanded state while he negotiated traffic and routes. Previously Christopher had been visited by Christ and St. Michael the Archangel, and included angel channeling as part of his psychotherapy practice. He also had a practical side that kept him grounded, even at times like this.

"Vera, why did you say in the prayer hall that now you understand why I'm afraid of Swamiji?" I asked after we were in the car.

"Didn't you hear what he said to that American guy who went up to him? First he said, 'Hello. It's nice to see you again.' Then they were talking about something, and I heard Swamiji say, 'I'll step on your head with my foot and crush it.' I guess he hadn't done something he was supposed to do, so Swamiji said he'd crush his head."

Our laughter had a tinge of fear.

"You warned us he was unpredictable," Samantha said. When we arrived at the hotel she said, "Gee, we've driven all this way. Tomorrow we have a whole day with nothing scheduled until six o'clock."

"Well, we're not that far from New Orleans. Maybe we should spend the day there.

When I woke up the next morning Vera and Samantha were still sound asleep. I meditated and slipped out to the pool, a turquoise jewel beside a grey parking lot. Invigorated and ready for whatever the day might hold after a good swim, I entered the hotel room to the sound of a hair dryer. Vera was at the sink grooming. Samantha sat in lotus on the bed, her eyes closed.

Vera whispered, "We're not going to New Orleans. We thought we'd go to the temple instead. We're meeting downstairs at noon."

When we ambled down to the lobby, a half hour late, Christopher was lounging on a sofa, his arm stretched along the beige couch back. He showed no trace of irritation at our lateness. His unfurrowed face bespoke either resignation or simple acceptance.

"Ready?" he asked. We walked out to the car.

"Well, so much for going to New Orleans and calling us at ten o'clock," Vera said. "I couldn't have gotten up anyway."

"I rolled over and looked at the clock around ten," Christopher said, "but I was in some kind of altered state. I wasn't asleep and I wasn't awake. I felt like Swamiji was working on me, re-organizing all the cells in my body. I couldn't move, so I just stayed in that in-between state until about eleven thirty."

"Well, maybe Swamiji was just arranging what each of us needed. I really needed to swim to get out all the kinks from driving and sitting cross-legged. Vera and Samantha needed to sleep, and Christopher, you obviously needed a cellular rearrangement."

CHAPTER 26

Interview with Swamiji

All men desire peace, but very few desire those things that make for peace.

— Thomas à Kempis

At the temple we saw R.K., who had alerted us about Swamiji's visit to the U.S. We sat down on the floor and joined him and his family at the lunch table formed by a strip of paper stretching the length of the room.

R.K.'s face was full of light, and he seemed happy to see us.

"Are you coming to Dallas to see Swamiji tomorrow?" R.K. asked.

"No, because Rao said the Dallas meeting is private."

"Swamiji's purpose in Dallas tomorrow is to discuss possibly having a tour there next year. I'm helping to organize the meeting this year. I want as many people as possible. The greater the interest shown, the greater the likelihood Swamiji will come. So, please, come if you can. I'll give you directions."

Spending more time with Swamiji was tempting. However, it would mean driving about thirteen hours in one stretch.

"I wish we could see more of Swamiji here in Louisiana," Samantha said.

I was surprised when a group audience of the four of us with Swamiji effortlessly arranged itself via Christopher's credit card.

"Swamiji prefers it if you have in mind a specific question or something you want help with. It's good to write it down," R.K. said.

I entered the temple just as Swamiji was entering in his pink sari. I stood facing the aisle formed by two lines of people at the entrance. Swamiji walked between them and passed me, our eyes level. His brief but powerful look seemed to go to the depths of my soul. Embracing the furthest points of the continuum of the Absolute, it was a reminder that there is no escape from *karma,* or from ultimate God realization.

We sat waiting our turn for a private interview. Rao called names and ushered people into a room for their audience. Some groups of as many as fourteen people went in like flocks of birds to meet with Swamiji.

Even with a wall separating us, the effect of his presence was powerful. When we heard the "Dallas group" called, Rao ushered us in. A young Hindu priest dressed in orange robes sat on the floor. Joy and innocence shone in his face. He began to perform a *puja* as preparation for our meeting with Swamiji. Brass *puja* accouterments were in front of him, a steady flame burning from one of the lamps. The scent of sandalwood grew strong. A pair of Swamiji's wooden sandals lay on the altar.

The priest's bubbling bliss created a feeling of playfulness as he proceeded with the ritual. He broke off four flowers from the large white chrysanthemum plant beside him, and handed one to each of us. He chanted in Sanskrit, then picked petals from a flower and dropped them onto a small brass tray beside a mound of red powder. He dipped a flower in water and shook it on each of us. Cool drops hit my eyelids, face, and hair. The chanting grew louder. My eyes were closed. The priest placed a red dot of *kum kum* powder on my third eye. He stopped chanting and said, "Now make a *sankalpa*. Make a silent wish to put at the feet of the guru."

At the end of the *puja* he motioned to us to bow and touch the sandals. Another door opened and an attendant gestured to us to enter the small room. Swamiji sat on a slightly elevated platform. We knelt on the carpeted floor before him. He smiled and seemed joyful. "How are you?" he asked.

Slightly disoriented, we nodded in silence. Swamiji seemed accustomed to people who were at a loss for words in his presence. He turned to Christopher who stared at him blankly. "How is your practice?" Swamiji broke the silence. I started laughing aloud, amazed that Swamiji, who had never met Christopher, was asking him about his psychotherapy practice. I soon realized Swamiji was referring not to Christopher's professional practice but to his spiritual practice. I regretted my gaffe.

"Fine," Christopher said. "I'd appreciate recommendations for any prayers or spiritual routines I should include."

"Pray Swamiji for help," he said.

Swamiji turned to Vera. "I'm having problems with my husband and sister," she said.

"Swamiji will take. Swamiji will take problems," he said.

He turned to me. "Would you help me with a relationship?" I said.

Swamiji's eyes rolled up toward heaven, as though he were enlisting assistance of higher beings. Or perhaps he was thinking, "Here we go again: another woman seeking happiness where it is never to be found—in the realm of the impermanent."

"Swamiji will bless," he said.

"And could you help me with my writing and music," I said quickly, trying to squeeze in this extra boon.

He waved his hand at me as if to say, "Enough, enough."

I felt greedy and small, and again had the feeling he didn't like me.

He turned to Samantha. "Will you help me to cross the ocean of *samsara?*" she asked, referring to getting beyond the transitory world's repetitive cycle of births and deaths to enlightenment.

"Of course."

He handed us each a medal hanging on a red string. The medal was inscribed with his initials. We bowed and left.

Outside the door, an attendant passed us a piece of fruit. The medal and fruit were our *prasad*. My apple was bruised, and I mused that I didn't like apples. Again, I felt small and remembered that *prasad* is to be accepted as most precious. The apple seemed like another little dart designed to deflate my ego and rid me of spiritual pride.

The surface level of the audience was a minimal aspect of the real exchange which was the infusion of grace and blessings that comes from Swamiji's focusing his attention on us. This infusion of energy from an enlightened being required integration, a gradual re-entry. I longed for quiet solitude to incorporate fully the energy that expanded my interior world, and so I drew all my attention from the external world to it.

We sat in silence together. In my mind's eye, I saw celestial beings, receiving yet another assignment from Swamiji. I imagined them hard at work, running the boiler room of the universe, engineers of nature directed to change the course of my life. The previous order was my life as it had been; the new order was the changed life awaiting me. A medical intuitive once said that the beings in the spirit world have personalities, moods, and facial expressions as distinct from one another as human beings have. These looked weary.

Christopher nudged me from my reverie. "It's almost six o'clock," he said. "Let's go to the main hall so we can get good seats for Swamiji's concert."

"O.K.," I said, though it felt too soon to move. I got up.

"You know, Christopher, I was afraid you weren't going to say anything to Swamiji when we were in there. When he turned to you, you just looked at him for the longest time."

"Well, once we got in the room with him, I realized that I was in a dilemma. The whole purpose of meeting with Indian saints is to get enlightened which requires going beyond the mind. Anything I said to Swamiji, any question would be with the goal of getting beyond my mind. Just by being in Swamiji's presence my mind was starting to dissolve. To ask a question would reverse the process and put me back in the mind I'm trying to let go of."

I laughed. "No wonder you hesitated."

As we opened the doors to the large hall, the peppery rhythm of *tabla* drums and the elongated sounds of the sitar greeted us. Swamiji was not there. His musicians were playing. The crowd was singing *bhajans*. The music was too loud and pulled me too much in an outer direction. After such deep silence, I felt delicate and raw in the large crowded room.

Almost an hour passed before Swamiji came onto the stage. He sat at the synthesizer. Seemingly irritated, he exchanged words with his attendants, stood up, and walked out. From the commotion outside, he seemed to be leaving.

"Swamiji has instructed everyone to continue singing," Radhakrishna said. I was hungry and wanted to go back to the hotel room. Instead, I waited for another hour for Swamiji. Then Radhakrishna returned to the microphone.

"Now everyone should queue up to go to the building across the street. Swamiji will give blessings there. Afterwards, return here for more *bhajans* before dinner."

It was clear that Swamiji would not be spending the evening with the group as planned.

Samantha turned to me, "Unpredictable, indeed!"

"Maybe Swamiji was mad because the sound system wasn't tuned properly," I said. "It still had the scratchy quality that was there last night. Really, though, I have no idea why he left so suddenly."

We joined the long line of people ambling across the street and into the temple. Swamiji stood in the center of the hall.

As in India, Swamiji seemed unconstrained by social niceties, impression management, or compunction to attend to the parade speeding past him. He talked to whomever, whenever, executing the will of God, who is no respecter of persons. As they approached for his blessing some devotees only got a glimpse of his back before being shooed on by attendants engaged in crowd control.

I once read that Swamiji said to a group:

They are crying: "Swamiji is not looking. Swamiji is not laughing." I can't attend all the time. I am very busy. I cannot ask daily: "Oh, my dear, how are you? Ha, ha, ta, ta, tu, tu." Kissing here, kissing there.

That is not my job. We are not used to this: "How are you? Good
morning; bye, bye; Did you have a nice dream?" We are not used to
so many words. Don't give me these habits . . . If you ask today, and
you ask tomorrow, what happens after four days if you don't ask?
Then depression. Love is pure love. We don't want misunderstand-
ing. (Sachchidananda Swamiji, Sri Ganapati, 1996, 44).

I dashed past without a glance from Swamiji. I remembered how
devastated I was by such lack of attention in India. I felt wiser now,
understanding that social interaction is the least important aspect of a
relationship with him.

His attendant Radhakrishna took the microphone to make closing
remarks. "I want to review the program for tomorrow. In the morning,
starting at seven o'clock, Swamiji will perform Sri Chakra *puja* and *puja*
to Ganesh. When you do *puja* to Ganesh it is like telephoning to
Ganesh." His pudgy thumb and pinky finger stretched from his ear to
his mouth. The audience laughed.

"You are saying, 'Hello, Ganesh. I am thinking of you. I love you so
much. Thank you for blessings. Thank you for removing all obstacles in
my life.'"

As we were driving back to the hotel, Christopher said, "Let's be in
the lobby at six thirty tomorrow morning for check-out so we can get to
the temple by seven, in time for the *puja*s."

There was a collective groan at the thought of awakening at dawn
and leaving so early.

"Christopher, you've been very patient with our less-than-precise
sense of time," I said.

"The female sense of time is why men have to fight wars," Christopher said. "If women fought they'd be late to the battlefield. There would
be no one there to do the fighting. The enemy would say, 'So, where's
the opponent?'"

We laughed at his gentle, but pointed humor.

"That was an amazing day today," Samantha said. "It's a good thing
we had the private audience with Swamiji. Otherwise, we wouldn't have
seen much of him."

"I agree," Christopher said. "There I was, just eating my lunch. All of a sudden I had my Visa card out, and I was charging a blessing!"

We laughed at ourselves. We were certain of the value of what we were doing. Still, by any conventional norm, our behavior was bizarre.

CHAPTER 27

Echoing Hearts

All things are possible until they are proved impossible.
— Pearl S. Buck

The next day I woke early to moaning sounds from Vera. When I looked over, she was asleep and silent. Then the moans started again accompanied by thrashing in the bed.

"She must be having a nightmare," I thought. My intuition was strong not to disturb her. The sounds subsided after a few minutes. At five-thirty the alarm woke her.

"Oh, my God. I was having this horrible dream," she said. "Swamiji was standing in front of me with little red flowers around his neck. He took his hands and opened my chest. Then he cracked open my thorax and started to rip out my heart. He disconnected it from the veins, arteries, and everything.

"'Swamiji, what are you doing? You can't rip out my heart. I can't live without a heart,' I was saying.

142

"Swamiji started laughing. He looked at me in his pink shawl and sari and just laughed. Then . . . it was horrible . . . he started devouring my heart. He was grabbing my heart in his hands and putting it in his mouth. He was eating it, and he was laughing!"

Vera's eyes closed, and she seemed to fall asleep again. A few minutes later she stood up, walked toward the bathroom, then hesitated and collapsed on the bed clutching her chest.

"I don't feel very well," she said. Coming from Vera who always minimized physical problems, this had to be a grave understatement.

"What's wrong?"

"It's my heart," she said. "Something's wrong with my heart. My blood pressure is very low." Because she had finished medical school, she knew how to diagnose what was wrong. Grabbing her wrist, I felt for a pulse. It was very, very slow—almost imperceptible. It became even fainter and skipped a few beats.

"Should I call an ambulance?" I asked.

"No," she said.

"Low blood pressure, low blood pressure," I thought with urgency, grasping for a treatment. This was an emergency, and I needed to do the right thing. Thoughts crept in about Vera dying and my trying to explain to the hotel staff and police that I had not murdered her. I spotted the pot of coffee next to the sink. I poured a cup and diluted it with cold water.

"Here, drink this coffee. It will raise your blood pressure," I said.

She drank it. I had my hand on her pulse. It became stronger and within a couple of minutes it was pounding vigorously. "I feel better," she said. Relief replaced her wan look.

It was a little after six, and *puja* was at seven. I jumped in the shower and threw on some clothes. I rolled my suitcase outside and parked it by the open trunk of our car, ready for leaving after *puja*. I wasn't fully over the trauma. Practically panting, I told Christopher about Vera.

"I thought I should call an ambulance, but after she drank some coffee to raise her blood pressure she was completely back to normal, as if nothing had happened. It's been a madhouse and it's only six thirty in the morning!"

He loaded the suitcase, saying "Uh-uh, uh-uh," using his soothing, non-judgmental tone suitable for mildly hysterical patients who mix real and imagined events.

Vera appeared looking sleek, the picture of health in her white linen pantsuit, tanned skin, and blond hair. As Christopher drove to the temple he turned to Vera, "Michael said you had a rough morning."

"Oh my God! I was lying there with my chest ripped open. Swamiji swallowed my heart like a snake swallowing a mouse. And he was laughing! I said, 'Swamiji, what did you do? I can't live without a heart. You just left me with a body. What can I do with a body and no heart?' Swamiji just laughed, and walked away.

"I said, 'Swamiji, I'm dying. I can't get up. I can't go to the *puja* this morning.' And I heard his voice. He said, 'You will come. You must.' He was very stern. So here I am. I can't believe I'm actually fine now."

We arrived at the temple before the crowd, sat up front on the beige carpet, and meditated. When I felt a palpable shift, like sinking to a lower depth of the ocean, I knew Swamiji had entered the room.

I opened my eyes and saw him on stage in profile. Draped in pink, he sat in lotus under a carved wooden archway before a flower-strewn altar. The flame from a brass oil lamp on the table barely stirred. Swamiji's presence is always powerful, but when he performs *puja*, the feeling of sacredness is even more profound. Swamiji moved his hands in slow motion in symbolic *mudra* gestures, Vedic code words said to call forth millions of angels. Every step, every movement, including the rhythm of his breath, seemed calculated and pregnant with meaning.

After the *puja*s, all eyes were on Swamiji. There was a hush of anticipation as the crowd waited for him to speak.

"You must do *puja* to purify your heart," Swamiji said. "When you do *puja* to Ganesh, he takes your sins and eats them." Swamiji motioned with his hands, as though he were throwing peanuts into his mouth. "*Swaha, swaha.*"

"Only meditation is not enough. You must also do *puja* in your daily life. The more it becomes your daily worship, the more you immerse yourself."

Swamiji's powerful presence blasted me once again, and with eyes half-closed I drifted in and out of awareness, lost in a place with no boundaries. I felt light coming through the top of my head.

"You don't know how to do *puja*." Swamiji stretched his fingers far apart, reached his hand out toward the audience and made a grabbing gesture. "But Swamiji knows, so Swamiji takes your heart . . . Swamiji takes your heart," he said, pulling his fist back, "and Swamiji eats it."

His words echoing Vera's experience in the hotel room plopped me back to earth. My eyes forced open as I landed with a thud. Vera's dream of Swamiji eating her heart and her subsequent cardiac crisis had upended my equilibrium then. Now the remnants of my emotional circuits began disintegrating into photons of light as I heard the words, "Swamiji takes your heart and eats it." I could feel myself slipping away again to a place beyond containment, where the container and contained are one. I yielded to this experience of transcendence.

The image of Swamiji devouring a human heart, like the Goya painting of Saturn devouring one of his children, was too rare and specific to be a chance coincidence. Swamiji had to have created Vera's experience in union with this teaching to the audience. The logic of his stretching time, space, and causality was beyond my capacity to understand. To some extent, the teaching linking Swamiji's eating our hearts to the importance of doing daily *puja* worship was also beyond me. Perhaps he deliberately created this bewildering coincidence as a cosmic explanation point to his instruction to do daily *puja*. Delivered with this punch, it could not have glided over our heads. Nor could we forget his instruction.

Swamiji talked more as I drifted in a timeless expanse, feeling too diffuse to integrate the duplicate reality I had just experienced.

"Today Swamiji listened to your prayers. During Ganesh *puja* Swamiji heard so many pleas for making sickness better. So, now Swamiji will make special medicine."

Like baby birds peeping extra-loudly at the promise of food, my aches and pains from days of sitting on the floor intensified at the promise of medicine.

Swamiji took a white rose garland draped on the arm of his golden chair, plucked a flower and placed it on a brass tray in his lap. He separated the ivory petals and ripped them into small pieces, dropping them onto the shiny tray in a slow, hypnotic tempo.

His composed expression tightened as if he were in pain. A blast of grey-white smoke billowed up, obscuring his hands. The petals had exploded! His eyes looked heavenward, his face drawn up, still taut. Swamiji's hands were producing grey ash, which poured out of them from nowhere.

The audience gave out a collective gasp. We realized we were witnessing a miracle. Time was suspended in that moment.

Radhakrishna took the microphone and with excitement and awe said, "Sri Swamiji is materializing sacred ash. He is materializing *vibhuti* from his hands."

I peered at Swamiji in the cloud of powdery smoke. He looked transfigured: intense, but somehow absent. He seemed to be sucking in power from another dimension.

Swamiji's face had this same expression in the videotape I had seen of him standing amid flames in a fire pit where he materialized a *lingam*, an elliptical stone that symbolizes Shiva.

While I witnessed this wonder of ash pouring from his hands, I felt all impurities wash away. There remained only a feeling of total innocence. Swamiji clapped his hands together to extrude more, and the ash cloud then swelled to beyond where he was sitting. Vera's mouth dropped open like a drawbridge, and her eyes widened. Later she described her reaction:

"The ash was coming from his hands, powder flying everywhere. I was sitting so close I could taste it in my mouth. Every skeptical part of me that had ever thought, 'that's just hysterical people's misperceptions' went away. I realized that all of my scientific training and learned skepticism had been a barrier to my confronting divinity in the flesh. I was transformed as the skepticism dropped away. I saw a different look in Swamiji's face. I felt fear and awe of his greatness. I saw God in front of me."

Swamiji, the cosmic pharmacist, stopped the stream, and with chestnut hands, mixed the white petals and ash together. Then, with utter detachment, he handed the platter to an attendant.

Radhakrishna said, "Now this sacred medicine will be passed around. Take only a small piece so there is enough for everyone."

I put a piece in my mouth. Though it tasted like rose petals stirred in an ashtray, I felt I had received Holy Communion; the white petals had been broken like bread, and Swamiji had added his essence to them. I swallowed it, and the feeling of sacredness within me grew. I felt gratitude to Swamiji for injecting the miraculous into my life with an immediacy I would never have dreamed possible. On a more mundane level, I later noticed that my back also felt much better.

Swamiji began playing music. I floated through a vast expanse without edges. Occasionally, I opened my eyes to see Swamiji swaying as he sang and played. The visual stimulation would push me over the edge, beyond the limits of my ability to process his light-emitting image, and I would quickly shut my eyes again.

The music stopped after a couple of hours. Radhakrishna went to the microphone, "This concludes our program today. Sri Swamiji will hand out a special sweet that is sacred to Ganesh as *prasadam*. Please make a single line."

A request for action in the physical world was an unfair demand, an assault on my expanded state. I felt like a genie whose being had escaped from my bottle and dispersed at a distance from it. Like a beer-bellied soldier being inspected by an army captain, I tried to suck my genie-being back into my corporeal boundaries. It still trailed outside of me when I felt the jostling of people standing overhead. I tried to dredge up the energy required to arise from my position on the floor. In a daze, and a little dizzy, I came to my feet and went where the pushing crowd directed me.

Some minutes later I stood before Swamiji. He looked jolly and bursting with energy as he handed me a coconut-raisin treat, which I popped into my mouth. The sweetness and chewy texture had a grounding effect, pulling me back to the world of sensation. At the same time I kept my heavenly feeling from his injection of divine energy into the food. He was passing out the sweets with speed and buoyant energy as the large crowd filed past.

I am always struck by the rare moments when I see Swamiji "in action" in the physical domain, rather than sitting before a large group as I usually see him. He is a study in full integration of the divine and the grounded. I had seen this in India when he took the angels for a jaunt to the zoo. The outing had grown in grandeur as the day approached, and an entourage of about seventy Indians accompanied us. Such a large group moving *en masse* would normally resist speed. Swamiji, however, set the pace as leader of the pack. We zoomed from animal to animal at such a rate that, panting for breath, I prayed the zoo was small and our tour would soon be over. Anemia and protein deprivation from my fear of eating in India may have put me at a disadvantage. Nevertheless, Swamiji demonstrated an Olympiad vigor that made me want to adopt all Indian dietary, daily routine, and Ayurvedic practices. Swamiji brilliantly exceeds the challenge of being in a body.

This same integration of body and spirit distinguishes Indian spiritual seekers from Western practitioners who have adopted Eastern spiritual practices. Too often the Westerners become wan and disembodied. Carl Jung noticed the full integration of mind and body in India. "It is quite possible that India is the real world, and that the white man lives in a madhouse of abstractions . . . Life in India has not yet withdrawn into the capsule of the head. It is still the whole body that lives . . . When you walk with naked feet how can you ever forget the earth?"

❧

The sunlight was blinding outside the prayer hall. Simple, practical decisions required constricting and focusing our expanded awareness.

Beyond words, we drove back to the hotel to pick up Samantha. She had stayed behind because she wasn't feeling well. I felt sad that she had missed Swamiji's miraculous materializing of ash from nowhere, and the opportunity to eat the medicine of rose petals and ash transmuted from his body. She had forgone the mind-blowing experience of hearing the words, "Swamiji takes out your heart and eats it," after Vera's parallel experience in the hotel room that morning.

Even during my month with Swamiji in India I saw nothing as boundary-breaking as the events of this morning. I mused about the ease of my life now vs. the pain I had endured at Mekedatu, such as freezing nights on the concrete roof, coughing while beetles crawled around my aching body. "No pain, no gain" seemed to be as fitting an adage for the world of Swamiji as the world of biceps building.

Perhaps Samantha's malaise and Vera's near-emergency that morning were more of Lord Dattatreya's tests.

CHAPTER 28

Recognizing the Destination Within

Peace is to be found only within, and unless one finds it there he will never find it at all. Peace lies not in the external world. It lies within one's own soul.

— Ralph W. Trine

We drove the thirteen hours to Dallas. A few hours' rest at Vera's apartment in Dallas still left us reeling with fatigue when we arrived at the devotees' home. Swamiji, wearing peach-colored robes, sat on a beige couch in the stark living room. On the floor by his feet, a vase was bursting with pale pink roses. A cloth painting of Ganesh hung on the wall beside him. An intimate group of fifteen people, mostly Indians, contrasted with the crowds of several hundred that usually surround Swamiji. Except for the powerful radiance of his presence, the image of was one of friends visiting someone's home.

I felt privileged as I walked up to Swamiji, though I was empty-handed; I had no flowers or other offering. I bowed down and then returned to my backjack. Once my body touched the seat, the rest of my being continued sinking into the depths of Swamiji's presence. I closed my eyes and sat in silence.

In the distance, I heard voices in a language I did not understand. It was Swamiji conversing in Telugu with those sitting near him. His presence had catapulted me to a place where the discriminative mind could not follow. Even if I had known the language, I could not have processed it. (Later I learned Swamiji was urging the use of an Indian Community Center for *puja*s and worship instead of for cultural events.)

Vera sobbed softly. Later she told me that in a moment of total surrender, she had offered her heart to Swamiji. Feeling his divinity was absolute, she whispered to him, "Why did you have to rip out my heart? I would have given it to you anyway." Her surrender began in the prayer hall when sacred ash was flowing from Swamiji's hands. It was complete as her tears flowed at this moment.

During Swamiji's private audiences upstairs, we sat in the garage. Vera laid herself out in the warm sun on the driveway where she rested and stared at the sky. I sat on the bedspread inside the garage with a circle of people. They chatted while I sat with eyes closed. Images of Swamiji kept coming to mind.

In India, my fear blocked full appreciation of his gentle presence. I had come to realize the deep kindness behind the difficult lessons he used to push me toward enlightenment.

As I mused, Rao appeared, motioning us to come into the living room.

"We're going to do *Pada Puja* with Swamiji," he said. "Hurry. He's coming down now."

I scurried to my feet and found a spot in the living room. Preceded by his immense aura, Swamiji floated down the stairs, and we all stood with bowed heads feeling the power of his presence as he passed us. He sat on the couch, and we sat on the floor. The haunting sound of Sanskrit chanting filled the air as the *puja* began. I floated on the Sanskrit phrases, which carried me far from the room full of people and deep into myself. I recognized again that Swamiji's presence was a catalyst that sent me far into the interior universe of the self. Through my closed eyes I discerned the distant image of lights moving in a circle, part of the *arati* ritual honoring Swamiji. I heard a woman's sobs mingling with the chanted Sanskrit. I was familiar with the phenomenon of overpowering emotions accompanying moments of sacredness. The *puja* ended in silence.

Lost in myself, merging with the silence, I remembered drifting in the vastness of space during Swamiji's meditation music in Mekedatu when I had seen him surrounded by the planets. His emanation of unperturbed peace and stillness orchestrated the movement and maintained the balanced interconnections of the planets.

Those standing in front of me began to prostrate themselves, forming an aisle as Swamiji passed. I shifted from my awkward half-kneeling position to lying face down on the rug. I felt Swamiji's presence near me. I opened my eyes and saw his brown feet before me. They were immobile. The skin was supple, the flesh plump and radiant. Beside them lay a gold coin, larger than a half dollar.

An Indian woman reached out and touched his feet. This, I knew, was rarely allowed because when his feet are touched he takes on the devotee's *karma*. Now, however, I felt his immobility as a form of permission. I was approaching Swamiji's feet, even though I still had a hard time looking him in the eyes. Following the example of the Indian hands on the rug, I reached out my hands. The gold coin symbolized a choice laid before me, a hint of the life I had chosen, of millions of decision points. It reminded me of the wisdom of those choices, evident in the treasure to which they had brought me.

I reached out and touched Swamiji's feet. I felt the confluence of all that is sacred in every religion, the core of the divine.

In the stillness of Swamiji's presence, I realized the unitary underpinning of my pilgrimages and visits to saints. In the silence, I recognized that my travels to India and distant holy places had only one destination—the depths of the Self.

CHAPTER 29

Another Incarnation of Dattatreya?

Mountains cannot be surmounted except by winding paths.

— Johann Wolfgang von Goethe

I had almost finished my book about Swamiji when R.K. informed me of another Avadoota of Dattareya, the divine triad Brahma, Vishnu, and Shiva in one presence. An *Avadoota* is an incarnation of the divine that is beyond all social conventions and, thus, is unpredictable.

R.K. had encouraged me in my pursuit of Indian spirituality, and I would often run into him at meetings where we sought the *darshan* of Swamiji, Ammachi, and Karunamayi. I appreciated his taste in saints, and I was all ears when he told me about Avadoota Sri Viswayogi Viswamji.

"People ask me why I go to see so many saints," R.K. told me. "I always say, 'I'm like a bee going for nectar. I go because I love their honey.'

"Another divine soul is coming soon from India to Dallas. He may even be in Austin. His name is Sri Viswayogi Viswamji. He is love, pure love—divine love."

R.K. gave me the contact information. Sri Viswamji, I learned, *would* be in Austin, but only for two hours.

On the designated day, I bought some roses, headed for the meeting and got hopelessly lost. I began feeling the fluster of time urgency, thinking that I might miss the meeting. As I was going around in circles, the clock ticked past the designated time for his brief stop. I realized that the purpose for meeting was to help me along my path to enduring peace, thus, it made no sense to disrupt my physiology with nervousness. If I was to meet Sri Viswaguru Viswamji, then I would, I figured. If not, then it was God's will. The freedom of calm acceptance replaced my frenzy even though I was still lost. Finally, I stopped and called the hosts for directions.

"Am I late?" I asked. "No. We just got a call. Sri Viswaguru is on his way from Dallas. He is in Waco now. He'll be here in about 30 minutes." My calm was justified: it seemed that I *was* destined to meet Sri Viswaguru.

A wooded area opened into a suburban subdivision where the large limestone house was located. In the living room, twenty Indian women sat on the floor on Oriental carpets. They wore beautiful saris, bright orange, and cobalt blue. Another was turquoise with embroidered flowers. Many of the women had children in their laps. Barely moving, they seemed calmer and better behaved than American children.

Three large arched windows stretched from floor to ceiling. The room was almost bare but for three rugs and an extremely large chair with a purple sari draped across it. To one side of the chair, two large silver vessels sat on a footstool covered with an Indian cloth. Beside it were several plates of fruit and three platters piled high with flowers. These were materials for a *puja*.

The kitchen had a waist-high wall with an opening between it and the living room. Behind were signs of busy and elaborate preparations. Large pots on the stove and various bowls covered with tin foil indicated that an Indian feast would be served. There is a tradition of serving food to all the guests when a saint visits a private home.

A built-in bookcase along one wall of the living room contained a collection of elephants—elephants dancing, elephants standing. There was also a statue of Ganesh, among other Indian sculptures. On the mantelpiece was a picture of Sri Viswayogi Viswamji. His face was thin and his eyes intense. His grey hair was long and wavy. To the left of his photograph, surrounded by some unfamiliar symbols was a full-body photograph of a man. I later learned that was his guru, Sri Wadekar Maharaj. Six low flames from wicks burning in oil rose from a circular silver container in front of each photograph.

I sat down on the floor and leaned against a wall. I did not want to talk. When I looked at the photograph of Sri Viswayogi, I got a message to sit in silence. I was the only American in the room. An Indian woman across the room looked at me and smiled, a gentle welcoming gesture. Many of the Indian women were speaking in Telegu or Hindi.

Just then somebody said, "Sri Viswayogi has arrived." We stood and formed two lines on either side of the door. Sri Viswayogi Viswamji sauntered through the door at a fast clip and flashed a huge smile. He emitted exuberant energy and a sense of fun. His wavy hair was wild and windblown, his movements free and uninhibited. There was nothing constricted about his spirituality—just fullness. I immediately liked him. He seemed like someone I knew very well. I felt I would not have to contain myself in any way, nor feign a subdued demeanor. He was very much his own person, and I was certain that he could handle the most expansive, uncensored parts of me. I felt we had an excellent understanding: I knew who he was, and he knew who I was.

Later I read, "Sri Viswamji throws us into a den of delusion, giving us an impression that we know Him, while, in fact, none can claim that he knows Him truly. In this sense He may be regarded as an incarnation of the power of delusion" (Ratnamohini, 2000). I wonder if everyone in the room had felt a similar sense of familiarity with him.

As he walked down the two lines of people, Sri Viswaguru Viswamji put his right hand on the head of each person. Being taller than he was by several inches, I bent over for him to touch my head, and I enjoyed it.

When he reached the end of the line, he turned without a word, went into the bedroom, and shut the door. We stood in silence, thinking he would be back shortly. When he did not, we sat down.

A retinue of five Indian men accompanied Sri Viswamji. Now there were almost as many men as women in the room. As I walked back to my spot against the wall, I was surprised to see R.K. He sat on the floor in a pale blue shirt and Western trousers. He had just come from Dallas with Viswayogi Viswamji. He practically shouted when he saw me and vigorously shook my hand.

When Sri Viswayogi Viswamji finally reappeared, he sat on the large chair in the center of the living room. It was very soft, wide, and low to the ground. He put his bare feet on a small footstool. The couple hosting the event knelt before Viswamji, chanted, and put flowers and rice on his bare feet. During the *puja*, a usually solemn event, Sri Viswayogi occasionally wiggled his toes as the power of the universe coursed through his body, demanding movement. Energy seemed to enter the top of his head and ripple through him like a raging river that cannot be contained.

Two things fascinated me: the massive amount of easily accessed energy he had, and his freedom to do whatever, wherever, whenever. I sensed that he would refrain from doing nothing that he wanted to do, unconcerned about the reactions of others.

Paroxysms of slapping broke the usual solemnity, as he burst into even more motion, hitting the padded arm of the chair repeatedly. His face turned up to the high ceiling, which he examined with apparent interest. With his other hand, he kept slapping his thigh in an accelerating frenzy; all of this as the humble couple chanted in Sanskrit and placed more and more flowers and rice on his feet. Sometimes it would be a few small slaps and then thunderous repeated slaps, as though he were playing a rhythm on *tabla* drums. It seemed not so much that he could not sit still, but that he choose not to. I sensed that he could lift huge rocks. I could not imagine this man ever being tired.

It is said that Sri Viswamji announced to his devotees that great quantities of energy are concealed within him, and everyone could draw whatever they needed. Out of compassion, he makes an infinitesimal amount of his power known to his devotees for their happiness. His true nature is primordial power and not the form that we see moving amongst us.

I prayed silently, "Please give me some of that energy. Show me how to have energy like yours."

Several times, he looked over and grinned at me where I sat against the wall. I smiled back at him and felt happy. At three different times during the *puja,* while looking me straight in the eye, he raised his hand in what was perhaps a blessing gesture. I later saw a poster of him with his hand in the same position. Light beamed out from the palm of his hand to the world. The caption read, "The Lord and the world are one. The universe shines in the Lord. If the Lord does not shine, the universe does not shine." Perhaps he was sending some of that light that holds up the universe.

As the hosting couple continued kneeling and chanting before him, he grabbed a banana and sliced it in half. He dipped the two cut ends in red *kum kum* powder (used for marking the third eye). Then he joined the cut ends of the banana together again. He seemed so distracted from the *puja* and so busy looking around the room and moving his hands, that his feet as sacred objects of worship seemed almost separate from the rest of his body. Midway through the *puja,* he again cut a banana, dipped the two ends in *kum kum* powder, joined them, and then dropped the banana pieces to the floor on each side of his chair. Meanwhile the pile of rice on his feet grew taller.

Later R.K. explained, "Through this action with the banana, he was invoking cosmic forces to minimize bad qualities of people in the room. Just as with good and bad cholesterol, you cannot convert bad cholesterol into good cholesterol. So with human beings, the goal is to maximize the good and minimize the bad. Although it is not possible to completely eradicate bad qualities and turn them into good qualities, bad qualities *can* be reduced to a low level." Sri Viswamji, like all other incarnations of Dattatreya, works for the welfare of humanity by eliminating the demonic tendencies and transforming people into better beings. In bringing about this transformation, his only weapon is love.

I later read more about his actions with bananas. A large group of devotees gathered outside for a ritual celebration in India. The sky darkened, and a downpour that would have inconvenienced all seemed imminent. Sri Viswamji looked at the sky, took two bananas, cut them in half, and placed camphor in each cut end. After lighting the camphor, he put each piece of banana in a corner of the area. The clouds cleared away.

After chanting the thousand names of Viswayogi, we stood up. Someone put a small handful of saffron-colored rice in each of our hands. Another person came by with a platter of flowers, and said to take one. They missed me, however.

"Women first, stand to the left. Go and place the rice and flowers on Sri Viswamji's feet and receive his blessing."

As I stood in line, I whispered to R.K. that I had no flowers to offer. He opened his hand and gave me some petals. "When you go up, tell him you want to talk to him privately. Tell him how you happened to come here today," he said.

I knelt before Sri Viswayogi Viswamji and placed the rice and flowers on his feet.

I really did not want to meet with him privately. I felt I had nothing to say, so I did not request a meeting. I simply wanted to enjoy the experience of being present with him. "R.K. told me about you. I would like to learn more about you."

Sri Viswayogi focused his eyes intently on me. Then, in a stern voice, he said, "Be happy." His voice was uncompromising, yet exuberant. "Be happy." It was a command, like "Stand up straight," or "Kneel down." It was non-negotiable. I liked that.

I have since read that although Sri Viswamji speaks briefly but pointedly to those who come to him, everything he says has importance, though we may not grasp it at the time. We may not realize their significance, but the words have deep inner meaning and prove true in time.

They have the same inevitability as the motion of planets. His words are Vedic commands with divine power and can render miracles.

R.K. said Sri Viswamji must have detected some area of unhappiness in me. And that, in saying "Be happy," he was taking the burden of what was troubling me.

I stood up from my brief meeting with Sri Viswaguru and realized that he was giving *kum kum* dots to others on their third eye. I had retreated too quickly to get one, and I feared I lost a blessing. When I mentioned this to R.K., he said, "Go back and ask him for one."

"What is it called?"

He said something like "dootu" or "dutoe."

I was flustered. I went back up, knelt down, and said, "dootu," mispronouncing the word. Sri Viswamji did not seem to understand my request. So, I said "dutoo," "doyu," thinking that some variant of the sound would have to be correct. The face of one of the Indian attendants brightened when he figured it out. He laughed, corrected my pronunciation, and Sri Viswayogi gave me my *pootu*, applying the red powder between my eyebrows.

Sri Viswayogi uses touch to turn devotees onto the path that leads to spiritual wealth, away from acquisition of material wealth and happiness, which are impermanent and bind the soul to the cycle of rebirths.

After anointing me, Sri Viswayogi, in an energetic flash, reached over the side of the chair and grabbed a bouquet of flowers. He presented it to me, practically shoving it at me with his rapid movements. I was surprised and delighted.

Sri Viswamji once put a garland of flowers around the neck of a devotee who asked for his grace. He told the devotee that it represented the grace of many lifetimes. In giving his grace, by giving flowers to a devotee, Sri Viswamji grants new energy for a virtuous life. I assume that Sri Viswamji was also granting me his grace this way. Sri Viswamji's acceptance of a flower garland from a devotee signifies that he accepts and takes on their *karma*, absolving them of its consequences.

"I didn't know he gave you flowers. That's very good," R.K. later told me. "That means that he has established a bond with you."

"Why?" I asked.

"You have something of his now. It is a means of connecting. Now you can call on him anytime. Distance is no barrier. He will know you are calling and he will help you."

I had occasion to test this some months later when I was in what felt to be a desperate situation. I called on Sri Viswamji and asked for his help. I remembered reading that whoever thinks of him and chants the mantra *Om Sri Sairam Gurudevadatta* will be sure to feel Sri Viswamji's instantaneous presence. The mantra is a cure-all medicine for devotees. The moment he receives the sound waves of his devotees' prayers from however far away, he rushes to them instantly and suggests solutions or solves their problem.

I silently repeated the mantra and asked him to PLEASE help me with the toxic situation in which I found myself, surrounded by people abusing drugs and alcohol in a city equally polluted with smog. I was at the airport within an hour, although it was the middle of the night. Minutes later, I was on a plane. In retrospect, leaving was the wisest choice. I do not think I would have acted as I did, and at such an hour, had Sri Viswamji not instantly catalyzed me to do so. He seemed to blast me with a bolt of his characteristic energy which overcame my exhaustion and moved me to a purer, more life-supporting environment.

After everyone had approached Sri Viswayogi and received his blessing, he again disappeared into the bedroom.

"Did you ask him for a private meeting?" R.K. asked.

"No, I didn't, because I don't really want a private meeting with him. I don't have anything to say."

"Ask him for blessings for your book and for publishing it." I thought this was an excellent idea. I convinced R.K. to come in with me, and told one of his devotee guards at the room that I would like to talk to Sri Viswayogi Viswamji privately. I said it would only take five seconds.

"All right," he said. "Go in after the next person comes out."

Sri Viswamji sat facing the door. I bowed and asked, "Could I have your blessings?"

"My blessings are always there," he said.

"But could I have blessings specifically for a book I want to publish?"

R.K. intervened and began talking in Telegu. He explained that I was writing a book about encounters with divine souls. He asked if I could have permission to describe the meeting with Sri Viswamji and to include a photograph of him. Sri Viswamji's face became more animated. He turned to me, looked up, and asked, "You are a writer?"

"Yes," I said. I loved being called a writer. His question felt like a statement, a recognition, a re-definition of my profession, bringing writing from the periphery to the center of my life. Although I wrote occasionally, I thought of myself primarily as a psychologist. Sri Viswamji often advises those coming to him to take up a particular course of study, sometimes contrary to what the person had in mind. He does this because he knows their abilities and their future. He foresees what is good for them, blesses and guides them accordingly.

Sri Viswamji is also a writer and has published a volume of poetry. At his ashram in India, he always shows great regard for poets, and encourages writers to present their work to an audience there. His own poems reflect his burning desire to reform humankind and to bring about unity in society.

R.K. was kneeling down. In Telegu, Sri Viswamji said that he blessed the publication and success of my book. I knelt down, too, at a distance. When they finished talking, I bowed my head, said "Thank you," and exited the room. "You told me it was going to take five seconds, but it only took three seconds," the guard at the door said. He laughed.

"So, do I get a bonus?"

"Yes," he said. "The next time you get fifteen minutes."

R.K. walked with me into the living room and over to a long-time devotee from India, who opened a travel-worn cardboard box. He handed me a poster with a photograph of Sri Viswamji, plus a book about him. Sri Viswamji had directed him, through R.K., to give me these items.

As he handed me the book, he said, "There is really only one God. There are three names, three forms, but it is only one God." He seemed to want to dispel any confusion that I, as a novice Westerner, might have about the concept of Dattatreya, the incarnation of the three main gods,

Brahma, Vishnu, and Shiva. But R.K. interrupted him in Telegu, telling him that I was a devotee of Swamiji Sachchidananda Ganapati.

His tone and expression suddenly changed from that of a slightly pedantic teacher to colleague. "Oh, then you *know* about Dattatreya," he said. "Swamiji and Sri Viswamji are in constant telepathic contact. Whenever they want to, they can communicate with each other, because they are both incarnations of Dattatreya, and both are tuned in to the cosmic mind."

As I was enjoying a delectable Indian meal replete with chutneys, dal, vegetables, and chapatis I talked to a woman from Kashmir who looked Celtic. I was surprised when she told me she was Indian. She said she was typical of many in Kashmir who are light-skinned and redheaded. She told me a little bit about the origin of her people: many Muslims in Kashmir are actually Hindus who converted because they didn't like the caste system in India. They thought they could achieve a better status by becoming Muslims, but they are really Hindus.

I sat quietly on the floor for a moment and thought about the day. It was, indeed, a different kind of feeling with this Dattatreya. The primary experience was enjoyment. Enjoy. Enjoy. Enjoy. That was the main word, his theme.

I said good-bye because it was time to go to work. As I left the house, I saw pieces of a broken coconut on the sidewalk in front of the entrance. Sri Viswamji's breaking of coconuts for no apparent reason is actually to drive away evil forces. Coconuts are auspicious signs of cosmic power. He once advised a devotee to give a paralyzed boy sacred ash and to break coconuts in certain places. After the devotee carried out the instruction, the boy miraculously showed movement in his leg. On another occasion, a devotee asked for help with a stalled construction project. Sri Viswamji instructed her to break a coconut in a particular part of the land. Once she did so, the builder immediately and unexpectedly came forward and arranged for the construction to begin.

Once in my car, I again got completely mixed up, not knowing which way I was going. I had trouble just getting out of the *cul de sac* where I parked. I then recognized that meeting with Sri Viswayogi was more powerful than I thought.

I went to work for a couple of hours, and it almost destroyed me. I was so exhausted that I wondered if I could safely drive home without falling asleep at the wheel. I went right to the meditation building in Radiance and lay down to rest before other people came in to meditate. I was out like a light. Three hours later, I woke up having missed the entire meditation. I was not concerned because I knew that something good was happening, something that required my conscious mind to get out of the way.

How could both Swamiji and Sri Viswayogi simultaneously be living incarnations of Brahma, Vishnu, and Shiva? I am still wondering. There is time to ponder this mystery because the spiritual path continually unfolds, the loose pieces never fully gathered.

Epilogue

*T*he saints have remained active in my life. For example, during a visit with Karunamayi in Sedona, Vera, with her unshuttable third eye, delivered a stern and precise set of directions for me from Karunamayi. They included a critique of the energy-blocking architecture of my house and instructions to rip out certain walls, to install a solarium, and other renovations according to Vedic architecture, which aligns the individual with Nature. Currents of energy now flow where walls used to be. The sacred space in the precise center of the house where, according to Vedic architecture, the God Brahma resides is free of the walls that were hindrances to unobstructed stillness. A new skylight allows Brahma's home access to the energies from above which gently whirl in and flow through newly installed arches throughout the house.

⊶⊰⊱⊷

Swamiji still provides the most challenging lessons. Known as the silent teacher who communicates clearly with his devotees on the inner planes, I once heard him tell me to "Take a bath!" It was during the extensive house renovations. Accustomed to showering, I almost never take baths. I was resistent most of the day, but his voice was insistent. Finally, and a bit begrudgingly, I got into the tub. The water turned a dirty gray. I can only assume that the dust in the air from months of renovations lodged in my pores. Presumably, the debris was unaffected by showering, but was extracted by soaking in hot water.

One morning a few days later I planned to spend the afternoon doing errands. Swamiji's voice sternly and urgently told me, "Go now! Go immediately." At first, I resisted, because I had not planned on going out until later in the day. However, Swamiji hit me with both barrels, practically screaming with intensity, "Now! Go now!" Recalling that I learned from my bath experience not to question nor disregard Swamiji's messages, I threw on my jeans and jumped in the car.

Puzzling about the urgent tone of the instruction, I drove for a while and wondered what possible reason there was to leave at that particular time rather than later in the afternoon. When I turned onto the congested highway, I put my foot on the brake as I approached a red light. To my horror, my foot went to the floor. There was no pressure whatsoever—I had no brakes. I tried pumping the brakes to no avail as I rolled downhill toward the red light. I panicked and slammed my horn on, hoping that the surrounding cars would realize something was wrong. Miraculously, the light turned green. I rolled through and then saw the T-intersection with another highway ahead. The only possibility of avoiding a multi-car collision was to cross two lanes to get to the side of the highway. I could steer but had no control of the speed of crossing. I aimed toward the side of the road and saw an eighteen-wheeler approaching in one of the lanes between me and the side of the road. The truck whizzed by seconds before I crossed. Another large truck followed. Somehow, I slipped between them, got to the embankment, and rolled up the hill toward a grove of trees. I recognized that I would crash into the trees but knew I had my seatbelt on and, at least, had avoided a multi-car collision. As I approached the trees, my car, ever-so-slowly came to a stop, perching on top of the hill, whose peak had captured the underbelly of the car.

Although shaken, I was completely unharmed. The seat belt had not even had to snap into action because the car had slowed so gradually to a stop. My heart pounded. Grateful for having averted disaster and my ambivalence quelled, I repeated, "Swamiji is my guru. Swamiji is my guru. Swamiji is my guru."

I feared that if I opened the door, the suspended car would flip over onto the roof. One of the truck drivers came to help me out, and called the police. The officer refused to write an accident report, stating there was no accident, just a malfunctioning part. A tow truck arrived. The driver saw that there was no way he could pull the car off its precarious position atop the hill. He called for a larger truck with a special scoop that could slide under the car and lift it. When it arrived, I was sitting on a grassy knoll counting my blessings.

I presume that as a guru can modify but not obviate *karma,* Swamiji sent the message to leave my house immediately, knowing that a split second difference in timing could have resulted in horrible injury. On hearing this interpretation, my sister was more skeptical and angry. Referring to Swamiji, she said, "I hate him. If he knew this was going to happen, instead of saying, 'Go now,' he should have told you not to go out of the house." My understanding, however, is that karma cannot be avoided, only modified.

Two years ago while visiting Swamiji I either fell or was attacked in a hotel room. I awoke in the night unable to figure out where I was, how I got there, or how long I had been there. I looked over and saw a photograph of Swamiji which anchored me. I remembered then that I had gone to see him, but still could not figure out in which city or in which country. I had a subdural hematoma, a condition associated with a 70 percent death rate. It required hospitalization and brain surgery. Not only did I survive, I am thriving.

After my next visit to Swamiji, who says his religion is music, my sudden desire to study piano again culminated in meeting a professor from the Department of Music at the University of Texas. Despite my limited talent relative to the virtuosos from all over the world who studied with her, she agreed to be my piano teacher. After a twenty-year hiatus from lessons, I was privileged to study Chopin, my great love, with her.

⋇

Ammachi continues her work in expanding my heart. Before visiting Ammachi, I sat crying with my dying pet of eighteen years. After she died, I immediately got on a plane to go see Ammachi, a visit planned long before the pet's illness. When I received *darshan,* Ammachi lifted all of my sorrow. Later during the weekend, I asked her about possibly switching to another job. She advised me to continue my work with the elderly, that it would be best for my spiritual growth.

⋇

I feel that Viswamji Viswaguru, the newest saint to enter my life, has been helping me with the completion and publication of this book, just as he said he would.

⋇

During a recent three-day silent retreat with Karunamayi I felt protected sitting inside with her, while thunder, rain, and lightning pounded the roof outside. As I sat meditating, I recognized this experience of safety amidst a furious storm as a metaphor for the saints: they provide a perpetual haven, granting protection and guidance, a buffer of comfort during the occasional storms of life.

RECOMMENDED READING

Amritasvarupananda, Swami. *Awaken, Children!*, 4 vols. San Ramon, California: Mata Amritanandaymayi Center, 1991-1993.

Devi, Bhagavati Sri Sri Sri Vijayeswari. *Blessed Souls: The Teachings of Karunamayi*, 3 vols, New York: Sri Matrudevi Visvashanti Ashram Trust, Inc., 1998-2001.

Krishnamurthy, Kuppa Venkata. *Sri Ganapati Satchidananda, Parts 1 and 2*. Mysore, India: Sri Ganapathi Satchidananda Ashram, 1993.

Jnanamritananda Puri, Swami. *Eternal Wisdom: Upadeshamritam, Volume 1*. Translated by Dr. M. N. Namboodiri. San Ramon, California: Mata Amritanandaymayi Center, 1997.

Jnanamritananda Puri, Swami. *Lead Us To the Light: A Collection of Mata Amritanandamayi's Teachings*. Translated by Dr. M. N. Namboodiri. San Ramon, California: Mata Amritanandaymayi Center, 2002.

Maharaj, Sri Nisargadatta. *I Am That: Talks with Sri Nisargadatta Maharaj*. Translated by Maurice Frydman. Durham, North Carolina: The Acorn Press, 1973.

Maharishi Mahesh Yogi. *Bhagavad Gita:: A New Translation and Commentary with Sanskrit Text, Chapters 1-6*. London: International SRM Publications, 1967.

Meera, Mother. *Answers*. Ithaca, New York: Meeramma Publications, 1991.

Paine, Jeffery. *Father India: How Encounters with an Ancient Culture Transformed the Modern West*. New York: HarperCollins Publishers, 1998.

Paine, Jeffery. *Re-enchantment: Tibetan Buddhism Comes to the West*. New York: W.W. Norton & Co, Inc., 2004.

Rao, V. V. Prakasa, comp. *Wonders of a Holy Master: Memorable Experiences of North American Devotees with His Holiness Sri Ganapati Sachchidananda Swamiji*. Mysore, India: Raga Ragini Trust, 1999.

Rao, V. V. Prakasa, comp. *Wonders of a Holy Master: Experiences of Devotees with His Holiness Sri Sri Ganapati Sachchidananda Swamiji, Volume 2.* Mysore, India: Raga Ragini Trust, 2001.

Ratnamohini, Dr. Smt. K., *Viswa Ratnamala.* Translated by Pemmaraju Ramagopala Rao. Guntur, India: ViswaMandir, 2000. (About Viswayogi Viswamji)

Roberts, Bernadette. *The Path to No Self: Life at the Center.* Boston: Shambala Publications, 1985.

Sachchidananda Swamiji, Sri Ganapati. *God Word II: Excerpts From Speeches by his Holiness Sri Ganapati Sachchidananda Swamiji.* Mysore, India: Sri Ganapathi Satchidananda Ashram, 1998.

Sachchidananda Swamiji, Sri Ganapati. *Sri Swamiji in Austria.* Mysore, India: Avadhuta Datta Peetham, 1996.

Sivaya Subramuniyaswami, Satguru. *Merging With Siva: Hinduism's Contemporary Metaphysics.* Hawaii: Himalayan Academy, 1999.

Sivaya Subramuniyaswami. *Loving Ganesa: Hinduism's Endearing Elephant-Faced God.* Hawaii: Himalayan Academy, 2000.

Venkatesananda, Swami. *The Concise Yoga Vasistha.* Albany: State University of New York Press, 1984.

Worthington, Gary. *India Fortunes: A Novel of Rajasthan and Northern India through Past Centuries.* Olympia: Time Bridges Publishers, 2003.

Worthington, Gary. *India Treasures.* Olympia: Time Bridges Publishers, 2003.

GLOSSARY

ABSOLUTE — The ultimate basis of all thought and being. Pure Consciousness; the unmanifest, unchanging, and transcendent Self God—the essence of man's soul; the timeless, formless, spaceless Primal Soul. The Absolute is beyond all relativity, beyond even the most subtle level of consciousness. Absolute Being; Absolute Reality; The Impersonal God; Brahman.

ACHARYA — A highly respected teacher. A title bestowed through ordination. A pontifical leader presiding over a monastery or *math* designated to safeguard Hindu teachings.

ARATI — "Light." The devotional circling or waving of a flame in a small lamp before a holy person or at the high point of a puja. Arati can be done as a brief puja.

ASHRAM — "Place of striving." Hermitage or retreat. A holy sanctuary and teaching center of a saint, swami, or guru.

AURA — "air," "breeze." The subtle energy field of light within and around a person, expressing their mental and physical state via its colors and vibratory rate. Highly evolved beings have auras of bright gold extending great distances, which give peace to all within its field.

AVADOOTA — A realized soul or wandering ascetic who is beyond all social convention and whose consciousness is equal to that of God. A special title bestowed on rare souls who live on earth but in a state of detachment, dedicated to their duty to bless and guide mankind toward enlightenment.

AVATAR — "Descent." An incarnation of a Deity into human or animal form. The Divine has descended innumerable times

170

in as many forms, of their own volition to accomplish a specific purpose. The most celebrated are Vishnu's incarnations as Rama and Krishna who came at the ends of the two previous *yugas*, or ages. Krishna, Vishnu's ninth incarnation, explained that, "Whenever *dharma* [righteousness] is in decay and *adharma* [nonrighteousness] flourishes, then I create myself. To protect the righteous and destroy the wicked, to establish dharma firmly, I take birth age after age." Bhagavad Gita, Ch. IV, v. 7 & 8.

AYIM SRIM HRIM — (Preceded by *Om.*) Powerful Goddess Saraswati mantra composed of four syllables, each with special powers.

AYURVEDA — "The science of life, or longevity." The traditional medical system of India based on balancing the energies at all levels.

BACKJACK — A lightweight, legless chair made for floor sitting, usually consisting of an aluminum frame covered with strong fabric.

BHAJANS — Songs sung in praise of God, entailing repetition of the names of God, usually sung in groups.

BHAKTI — The path of devotion, based on the supremacy of Divine Love.

CHAKRAS — "wheel," "circle." Centers of subtle energy, "*kundalini*." There are six major chakras in the human subtle body and one above the crown. Self-realization occurs when the *kundalini* uncoils from its dormant state at the base of the spine in the first, or root, chakra and travels up through the other five to unite in bliss with the seventh, or crown, chakra.

DARSHAN — "vision," "sight." Seeing with veneration; being in the auspicious presence of holy persons or divinities, inwardly or outwardly, with the desire/intention to receive their grace or blessing.

DHARMA — "to hold, sustain, carry." The invincible power of nature which upholds existence. Dharma maintains evolution and is the basis of cosmic life; it supports all that is evolutionary by creating positive results, and discourages all that is not via negative consequences. Variously defined as Divine Law, truth, virtue, righteousness, duty, responsibilities and obligations, that which upholds cosmic, social, and individual order. The rules and laws which help maintain general morality and govern religious communities. For the soul, *dharma* is actions that bring about the most spiritual progress. (See *Avatar.*)

DHOTI — A traditional loincloth worn by Hindu men, made from a long cloth wrapped around the lower part of the body, sometimes passed through the legs, and tucked in at the waist. Can be worn long as a skirt.

GAJAKESURI — Configuration of planets in the horoscope indicating a comfortable, kingly life.

GANESH — "Lord of Attendants (*ganas*)," also called "Ganapati." One of the Great Gods (*Mahadevas*), the beloved elephant-faced god, son of Shiva and Parvati; the Remover of Obstacles, and the Protector of Women and Travelers. As the Gateway to the Gods, Ganesh is invoked at the beginning of any endeavor, and before invoking any of the other gods. He is revered for his wisdom. He knows each soul's karma and their perfect path to success. He is easy to approach.

GHEE — Clarified butter, burned in lamps for worship, used also in cooking and in Ayurvedic medicine.

GURU — "The Venerable" or "Weighty One." A spiritual teacher with the authority of great knowledge or skill, who leads the follower from ignorance to true knowledge along the path to enlightenment.

GURU POORNIMA — "Fullness of the Guru." Full moon in July when followers honor the guru with some ceremony, usually with a *puja* or a *padapuja*, and rededicate themselves to everything the guru represents.

JYOTISH — "The study of light (stars)." The traditional system of Indian astrology known for its accurate predictive value.

KALI YUGA — The Age of Ignorance. The last and shortest of the four *yugas*, or ages, that comprise one *kalpa*, or eon. It is characterized by diminished virtue, ignorance, and injustice, and is the age in which we are currently living.

KALKI — "The white horse." The coming tenth incarnation of Vishnu, the Maintainer of the Universe, who manifests at the end of every age. It is expected that Kalki will arrive at the end of the current Kali Yuga. (See *Avatar.*)

KARMA — a) Physical or mental action; b) the principle of cause and effect; c) the consequence of action; d) the total of all of an individual's actions in this and previous lives. This important Hindu principle says that every action and thought has consequences, which will manifest eventually. This is expressed in the West as, "As you sow, so shall you reap" or, "What goes around, comes around," or, from physics as, "For every action, there is an equal and opposite reaction."

KARUNA — Compassion.

KARUNAMAYI — One who is full of compassion. Spiritual teacher with a beautiful singing voice who embodies Saraswati, the Goddess of Speech, Learning, and the Arts.

KUM KUM — Red powder made by mixing turmeric and lime. Considered auspicious, it is used in pujas to worship deities, and to create a dot, a *pootu*, on the forehead between the eyebrows, the "third eye."

LINGA or lingam — "Mark," "Token," "Sign of Shiva." A rounded, elliptical, sculpted or natural stone which represents Lord Shiva. Symbolic of his inexpressible nature, it is the simplest and oldest representation of the God, and the one under which he is most often worshipped. They can be sculpted from black stone, marble, metal, precious gems, crystal, wood, earth, or temporary materials, such as ice. The linga as the embodiment of Lord Shiva is found in virtually every Shiva temple.

MA — Mother, usually referring to a goddess.

MAHARISHI MAHESH YOGI — Great seer and saint who brought Transcendental Meditation to the West. A trained physicist, he discovered the principle of physics named after him, "the Maharishi Effect," which states that when the square root of one percent of a system becomes coherent, the whole system becomes coherent. Already established for physical systems, he has used it to good effect on the social level to calm down global hotspots, and to do research in the U.S. in the 1970s by gathering groups of TM meditators and siddhas to practice together in an area. Use of the principle continues to expand to help bring about world peace and an age of enlightenment.

MALA — A garland; a rosary or string of beads for counting prayers, usually made from *rudraksha,* sandalwood, or crystal.

MANTRA — *Man,* "to think;" *tra,* "to protect or liberate." A "mystical formula" usually from scripture—a sound, word, or phrase that has special power. Repeating the mantra sets up vibrations that purify the seeker at all levels, leading to a state free of thoughts and to union with the Absolute.

MATHS — Monasteries first established in India with goal of preserving and propagating Hindu teachings. The pontifical head of a *math* is called an *acharya.*

MAYA — Illusion; the entire creation; the creative force, the principle of creation always in process. Maya is the Goddess who, as the energy of Brahman, creates the Universe, then draws the veil of illusion over Reality so that we only see diversity. Thus spawns the ignorance which causes attachment and bondage.

MUDRA — "seal." Esoteric hand gestures that express specific energies or powers. Usually accompanied by precise visualizations, mudras are a vital element of ritual worship, dance, and yoga.

OM — The "cosmic hum" from which all other sounds and the universe itself emerge. This mystical syllable is the most sacred and auspicious of mantras, and is considered to be the distillation of the universe into sound.

ORGANIZING POWER OF NATURE — The subtle intelligence which structures, coordinates, and maintains the functioning of the universe with all its elements and forces.

PADA PUJA — *Pada,* "the foot." The sacred ceremony (*puja*) traditionally honoring the feet of the guru, usually represented by his or her sandals.

PADMASANA — *Padma,* "lotus;" *asana,* "posture." A cross-legged posture in which the feet are placed on the opposite thighs. The lotus pose, the most recognized hatha yoga posture and the best one for meditation since it calms and balances the intellectual and emotional energies.

PANDIT — "Learned one." A title given to religious scholars and theologians who are also well versed in philosophy and other related subjects.

POONYA — Credit or merit from the sum of good deeds performed in this or previous lifetimes.

POORVAPOONYA — Past life credit resulting from benevolent deeds performed in past lives, resulting in benefits destined to appear in this lifetime.

POOTU — A dot placed between the eyebrows, marking the third eye.

POORNA — whole, complete, full.

PRANA — *Pran*, "to breathe." Vital energy or life-giving energy.

PRANAYAMA — *Prana + yama*: "control." Breath control, a technique for regulating the breath. Since the breath is closely connected with the mind, controlling the breath leads to control of the mind and thoughts.

PRASAD, PRASADAM — "clarity," "brightness," "grace." a) The blessing of serenity and graciousness. b) An offering of food to a divinity or a guru. The blessed remains are shared with the attendees at the offering.

PUJA — A ritual of offering fruit, water, incense, flowers, etc., as devotional worship to a deity or guru. The ceremony can be brief or elaborate. The purpose is to purify the atmosphere around the deity, to establish a connection with the inner worlds, gain favor, and invoke the presence of the deity or guru.

RUDRAKSHA — The reddish brown seeds from fruits of the rudraksha shrub, regarded as sacred to Lord Shiva (*Rudra*). Worn singly or on a string as a rosary for counting prayers, they symbolize Shiva's love and compassion for humanity. It is said that when the god looked down and saw man's sorrowful plight, he shed a tear, which fell to earth and sprouted into the first rudraksha tree.

SADHANA — Spiritual practices on the path of Self-Realization. Self-effort, spiritual disciplines, the way to attainment of the goal. Regular practice builds strength of will, faith, and confidence, not only in oneself, but also in God and the guru.

SALAGRAMA — An ammonite—the coiled, flat, chambered black fossil of an extinct mollusk—from a river in Nepal; considered a sacred symbol of Vishnu, the Sustainer of the Universe.

SAMADHI — *"Standing within one's Self."* The state of true yoga: a state of consciousness beyond waking, dreaming, and deep sleep states, that of union with the object of meditation, the Supreme or the Absolute.

SAMSARA — The cycle of birth, death, and rebirth; the transient world; the sum of all the successive incarnations of a soul.

SAMSKARAS — a) Psychological tendencies from experiences in this and previous lives, the sum total of which form one's character. b) Rites of passage, marking major transitions in life (such as, birth, coming of age, betrothal, and marriage) bringing with them inner and outer benefits.

SANKALPA — Mental resolve, firm intention, solemn vow. The mental and verbal preparations before performing a sacred ritual. Once *sankalpa* is made, one is bound to complete the rite or worship.

SANSKRIT — "Perfect, complete." The ancient, sacred language of India from which most modern Indo-European languages originate. It is the language of nature in which the sound perfectly names the form, and is considered the exact communication vehicle between the earthly and celestial worlds. Sanskrit provides terminology for concepts not found in European languages. The Vedas, the Upanishads, all the Hindu holy texts were revealed in Sanskrit which is still used for these texts and for sacred rituals.

SARASWATI DEVI — "Elegant; One who flows." Goddess of Knowledge, Speech, and the Arts; the consort, or *shakti* (power) of the Creator Brahma; Mother of Creation. In her hands are the Vedas, the path to liberation, and the *vina* (a stringed instrument), because she is the origin of the Primal Sound from which creation springs. She wears white and rides a white swan, symbols of her purity. Devotees pray to her for learning, culture, and refinement in the arts. The River Saraswati is considered a personification of her.

SARI — The traditional garment worn by women in India, Pakistan, and other parts of South Asia, consisting of five to six yards of light fabric wrapped around the waist to create a skirt, and draped over the shoulder or head.

SATCHIDANANDA or SACHCHIDANANDA — *Sat*, "pure;" or "light,"—that which always was, is, and always will be; *Chit*, "consciousness;" *Ananda*, "bliss." Pure Bliss Consciousness—a combination of the three main qualities of the infinite, attributeless, and indescribable Absolute.

SELF — That which lies at the core of every soul, the essence of man's soul, namely God's perfection of Absolute Reality. An expression of complete identity, the liberated self merging without trace into the unmanifest, inexpressible Absolute.

SELF-REALIZATION — Direct knowing of God; a state of union with God; "ecstasy without form or seed" [seed = impression to spur future action]. Experienced as a change in perspective, a total transformation in which one understands the Truth which surpasses all understanding.

SEVA — "Service." Service as part of a spiritual path; one serves without thought of personal gain.

SUKASANA — Any easy sitting yoga posture; specifically, sitting cross-legged with feet tucked under the knees.

SWAHA — Goddess of Fire. Swaha is the mantra of consecration to the

Divine, particularly as the inner or spiritual fire of awareness. The mantra is repeated as offerings are made during *pujas* or *yagyas*.

SWAMI — "Lord, owner, self-preserved." A respectful title for one who knows or is master of himself, usually belonging to a Hindu monk who is completely dedicated to religious life.

SWAMIJI — The suffix "-ji" indicates affection.

TABLA — Small hand drums of India, one usually larger than the other and made of metal, with the smaller one made of wood.

TAMASIC — *Tamas*-like. *Tamas* is the third of the three fundamental qualities (*gunas*) of Nature, and is characterized by inertia, or sluggishness, darkness, and ignorance.

TAPAS — "Heat," "burning," "ardor," "glow." "Warming up the Absolute" by spiritual purification and an intense desire for union with God. Creating psychic or spiritual energy through austerities, penance, ascetic practices, such as fasting, intense meditation, and 108 prostrations, etc.; emphasizing the spiritual aspects of life by toning down or mortifying the physical levels.

TATTVA — Essence, thatness, or essential nature. The basic elements or principles of existence; the most subtle building blocks of creation. The unfolding of the universe proceeds from subtle to gross levels of *tattvas*.

TAT TVAM ASI — "That alone you are. You are That only." The teaching that God and you are not two, but one. And that That alone is liberation.

THIRD EYE — Located between the eyebrows, the sixth chakra (*ajna*), which gives "divine sight;" the seat of consciousness.

TULASI — Holy basil (*ocimum sanctum*). Held sacred because it is associated with the presence of Vishnu, and is considered to be the incarnation of his consort, the Goddess Lakshmi. Every pious house would have a sacred basil plant.

VATA — "fluctuation." The air element in the body and in the natural world. In Ayurveda, "The Science of Life," (one of the oldest systems of health, originating in India) the humors are called *doshas*. *Vata dosha* is the air humor. It is the principle of circulation and governs breathing and movement, as well as metabolic and nerve energy.

VEDAS — "Wisdom." The four sacred books of hymns, formulas, and revelation, forming the most ancient and authoritative scriptures which are the foundation of Hinduism. They were divinely revealed as sound to seers (*rishis*). The most important, longest, and oldest book is the *Rig* ("mantra") *Veda*. Two of the other Vedas, *Yajur* and *Sama*, derive from the Rig Veda. They sing in praise of the powers of nature as deities. The fourth and later book, *Atharva Veda*, centers on gaining success in material life. "Vedic" refers to the Vedas.

VIBHUTI — Sacred ash from the fire sacrifice, or *homa*, charged with divine power. Taken as medicine or worn on the forehead to confer blessing and protection.

YAJNA, YAGYA — "worship sacrifice." Ritual worship in which oblations, such as ghee, grains, flowers, etc., accompanied with chanting, are offered into a fire. *Agni*, as fire, delivers the sacrifice and prayers to the Deity.

YANTRA — A sacred diagram inscribed with mantras and triangles or other geometric figures. They may be etched on small metal plates, or may be three-dimensional in stone, crystal, or metal. They are used to focus one's energies according to the pattern, which may be for health, wealth, childbearing, or invoking a deity, etc. They can also placed in corners of a room to emit the energy of the deity represented.

YOGA — "union." *Yuj*, "to yoke or join." The path of yoking the individual with the transcendent or divine consciousness. The most familiar systems of yoga are, 1) *hatha*, physical postures for preparation for meditation, 2) *kriya*, breath control, 3) *karma*, selfless service, 4) *bhakti*, devotional practices.

YOGABRASHTA — Attainment of a high state of yoga in a previous lifetime followed by its willful destruction.

To order additional copies of this book

online contact

www.spiritwingspublishing.com

by mail
send check or money order for $27.00
(includes tax and shipping)
to

Spirit Wings Publishing
P.O. Box 92694
Austin, Texas 78737

To arrange speaking engagements
please contact the author at

nellocal@webtv.net